The Art of Interior Decoration

Grace Wood and Emily Burbank

The Art of Interior Decoration

Copyright © 2020 Bibliotech Press
All rights reserved

The present edition is a reproduction of previous publication of this classic work. Minor typographical errors may have been corrected without note, however, for an authentic reading experience the spelling, punctuation, and capitalization have been retained from the original text.

ISBN: 978-1-64799-187-6

PLATE I

There is something unusually exquisite about this composition. You will discover at a glance perfect balance, repose—line, everywhere, yet with it infinite grace and a winning charm. One can imagine a tea tray brought in, a table placed and those two attractive chairs drawn together so that my lady and a friend may chat over the tea cups.

The mirror is an Italian Louis XVI.

The sconces, table and chairs, French.

The vases, Italian, all antiques.

A becoming mellow light comes through the shade of deep cream Italian parchment paper with Louis XVI decorations.

It should be said that the vases are Italian medicine jars—literally that. They were once used by the Italian chemists, for their drugs, and some are of astonishing workmanship and have great intrinsic value, as well as the added value of age and uniqueness.

The colour scheme is as attractive as the lines. The walls are grey, curtains of green and grey, antique taffeta being used, while the chairs have green silk on their seats and the table is of green and faded gold. The green used is a wonderfully beautiful shade.

Portion of a Drawing Room, Perfect in Composition and Detail

FOREWORD

If you would have your rooms interesting as well as beautiful, make them say something, give them a spinal column by keeping all ornamentation subservient to line.

Before you buy anything, try to imagine how you want each room to look when completed; get the picture well in your mind, as a painter would; think out the main features, for the details all depend upon these and will quickly suggest themselves. This is, in the long run, the quickest and the most economical method of furnishing.

There is a theory that no room can be created all at once, that it must grow gradually. In a sense this is a fact, so far as it refers to the amateur. The professional is always occupied with creating and recreating rooms and can instantly summon to mind complete schemes of decoration. The amateur can also learn to mentally furnish rooms. It is a fascinating pastime when one gets the knack of it.

Beautiful things can be obtained anywhere and for the minimum price, if one has a feeling for line and colour, or for either. If the lover of the beautiful was not born with this art instinct, it may be quickly acquired. A decorator creates or rearranges one room; the owner does the next, alone, or with assistance, and in a season or two has spread his or her own wings and worked out legitimate schemes, teeming with individuality. One observes, is pleased with results and asks oneself why. This is the birth of Good Taste. Next, one experiments, makes mistakes, rights them, masters a period, outgrows or wearies of it, and takes up another.

Progress is rapid and certain in this fascinating amusement,—study—call it what you will, if a few of the laws underlying all successful interior decoration are kept in mind.

These are:

HARMONY
in line and colour scheme;

SIMPLICITY
in decoration and number of objects in room, which is to be dictated by usefulness of said objects; and insistence upon

SPACES
which, like rests in music, have as much value as the objects dispersed about the room.

Treat your rooms like "still life," see to it that each group, such as a table, sofa, and one or two chairs make a "composition," suggesting comfort as well as beauty. Never have an isolated chair, unless it is placed against the wall, as part of the decorative scheme.

In preparing this book the chief aim has been clearness and brevity, the slogan of our day!

We give a broad outline of the historical periods in furnishing, with a view to quick reference work.

The thirty-two illustrations will be analysed for the practical instruction of the reader who may want to furnish a house and is in search of definite ideas as to lines of furniture, colour schemes for upholstery and hangings, and the placing of furniture and ornaments in such a way as to make the composition of rooms appear harmonious from the artist's point of view.

The index will render possible a quick reference to illustrations and explanatory text, so that the book may be a guide for those ambitious to try their hand at the art of interior decoration.

The manner of presentation is consciously didactic, the authors believing that this is the simplest method by which such a book can offer clear, terse suggestions. They have aimed at keeping "near to the bone of fact" and when the brief statements of the fundamental laws of interior decoration give way to narrative, it is with the hope of opening up vistas of personal application to embryo collectors or students of periods.

CONTENTS

	FOREWORD	v
CHAPTER I	HOW TO REARRANGE A ROOM *Method of procedure.—Inherited eyesores.—Line.—Colour.—Treatment of small rooms and suites.—Old ceilings.—Old floors.—To paint brass bedsteads.—Hangings.—Owning two or three antique pieces of furniture, how proceed.—Appropriateness to setting.—How to give your home a personal quality.*	1
CHAPTER II	HOW TO CREATE A ROOM *Mere comfort.—Period rooms.—Starting a collection of antique furniture.—Reproductions.—Painted furniture.—Order of procedure in creating a room.—How to decide upon colour scheme.—Study values.—Period ballroom.—A distinguished room.—Each room a stage "set."—Background.—Flowers as decoration.—Placing ornaments.—Tapestry.—Tendency to antique tempered by vivid Bakst colours.*	10
CHAPTER III	HOW TO DETERMINE CHARACTER OF HANGINGS AND FURNITURE-COVERING FOR A GIVEN ROOM *Silk, velvet, corduroy, rep, leather, use of antique silks, chintz.—When and how used.*	22
CHAPTER IV	THE STORY OF TEXTILES *Materials woven by hand and machine, embroidered, or the combination of the two known as Tapestry.—Painted tapestry.—Art fostered by the Church.—Decorated walls and ceilings, 13th century, England.*	26

CHAPTER V	CANDLESTICKS, LAMPS, FIXTURES FOR GAS AND ELECTRICITY, AND SHADES	
	Fixtures, as well as mantelpiece, must follow architect's scheme.—Plan wall space for furniture.—Shades for lights.—Important as to line and colour.	30
CHAPTER VI	WINDOW SHADES AND AWNINGS	
	Coloured gauze sash-curtains.—Window shades of glazed linen, with design in colours.—Striped canvas awnings.	34
CHAPTER VII	TREATMENT OF PICTURES AND PICTURE FRAMES	
	Selecting pictures.—Pictures as pure decoration.—"Staring" a picture.—Restraint necessary in hanging pictures.—Hanging miniatures.	37
CHAPTER VIII	TREATMENT OF PIANO CASES	
	Where interest centres abound piano.—Where piano is part of ensemble.	41
CHAPTER IX	TREATMENT OF DINING-ROOM BUFFETS AND DRESSING-TABLES	
	Articles placed upon them.	43
CHAPTER X	TREATMENT OF WORK TABLES, BIRD CAGES, DOG BASKETS, AND FISH GLOBES	
	Value as colour notes.	44
CHAPTER XI	TREATMENT OF FIREPLACES	
	Proportions, tiles, andirons, grates.	46
CHAPTER XII	TREATMENT OF BATHROOMS	
	A man's bathroom.—A woman's bathroom.—Bathroom fixtures.—Bathroom glassware.	47
CHAPTER XIII	PERIOD ROOMS	
	Chiselling of metals.—Ormoulu.—Chippendale.—Colonial.—Victorian.—The art of furniture making.—How to hang a mirror.—Appropriate furniture.—A home must have human quality, a personal note.—Mrs. John	

	L. Gardner's Italian Palace in Boston.—The study of colour schemes.—Tapestries.—A narrow hall.	54
CHAPTER XIV	PERIODS IN FURNITURE	
	The story of the evolution of periods.—Assyria.—Egypt.Greece.—Rome.—France.England.America.—Epoch-making styles.	59
CHAPTER XV	CONTINUATION OF PERIODS IN FURNITURE	
	Greece.—Rome.—Byzantium.—Dark Ages.—Middle Ages.—Gothic.—Moorish.—Spanish.—Anglo-Saxon.—Cæsar's Table.—Charlemagne's Chair.—Venice.	62
CHAPTER XVI	THE GOTHIC PERIOD	
	Interior decoration of Feudal Castle.—Tapestry.—Hallmarks of Gothic oak carving.	64
CHAPTER XVII	THE RENAISSANCE	
	Italy.—The Medici.—Great architects, painters, designers, and workers in metals.—Marvellous pottery.—Furniture inlaying.—Hallmarks of Renaissance.—Oak carving.—Metal work.—Renaissance in Germany and Spain.	65
CHAPTER XVIII	FRENCH FURNITURE	
	Renaissance of classic period.—Francis I, Henry II, and the Louis.—Architecture, mural decoration, tapestry, furniture, wrought metals, ormoulu, silks, velvets, porcelains.	69
CHAPTER XIX	THE PERIODS OF THE THREE LOUIS	
	How to distinguish them.—Louis XIV.—Louis XV.—Louis XVI. Outline.—Decoration.—Colouring.—Mural Decoration.—Tapestry.	74
CHAPTER XX	CHARTS SHOWING HISTORICAL EVOLUTION OF FURNITURE	
	French and English.	81

CHAPTER XXI	THE MAHOGANY PERIOD *Chippendale.—Heppelwhite.—Sheraton.—The Adam Brothers.—Characteristics of these and the preceding English periods; Gothic, Elizabethan, Jacobean, William and Mary, Queen Anne.—William Morris.—Pre-Raphaelites.*	86
CHAPTER XXIII	THE COLONIAL PERIOD *Furniture.—Landscape paper.—The story of the evolution of wall decoration.*	93
CHAPTER XXII	THE REVIVAL OF DIRECTOIRE AND EMPIRE FURNITURE *Shown in modern painted furniture*	95
CHAPTER XXIV	THE VICTORIAN PERIOD *Architecture and interior decoration become unrelated.—Machine-made furniture.—Victorian cross-stitch, beadwork, wax and linen flowers.—Bristol glass.—Value to-day as notes of variety.*	98
CHAPTER XXV	PAINTED FURNITURE *Including "mission" furniture.—Treatment of an unplastered cottage.—Furniture, colour-scheme.*	100
CHAPTER XXVI	TREATMENT OF AN INEXPENSIVE BEDROOM *Factory furniture.—Chintz.—The cheapest mirrors.—Floors.—Walls.—Pictures.—Treatment of old floors.*	102
CHAPTER XXVII	TREATMENT OF A GUEST ROOM *Where economy is not a matter of importance.—Panelled walls.—Louis XV painted furniture.—Taffeta curtains and bed-cover.—Chintz chair-covers.—Cream net sash-curtains.—Figured linen window-shades.*	106
CHAPTER XXVIII	A MODERN HOUSE IN WHICH GENUINE JACOBEAN FURNITURE Is APPROPRIATELY SET *Traditional colour-scheme of crimson and gold.*	110

CHAPTER XXIX	UNCONVENTIONAL BREAKFAST-ROOMS AND SPORTS BALCONIES	
	Porch-rooms.—Appropriate furnishings.—Colour schemes.	113
CHAPTER XXX	SUN-ROOMS	
	Colour schemes according to climate and season.—A small, cheap, summer house converted into one of some pretentions by altering vital details.	116
CHAPTER XXXI	TREATMENT OF A WOMAN'S DRESSING-ROOM	
	Solving problems of the toilet.—Shoe cabinets.—Jewel cabinets.—Dressing tables.	120
CHAPTER XXXII	THE TREATMENT OF CLOSETS	
	Variety of closets.—Colour scheme.—Chintz covered boxes.	123
CHAPTER XXXIII	TREATMENT OF A NARROW HALL	
	Furniture.—Device for breaking length of hall.	124
CHAPTER XXXIV	TREATMENT OF A VERY SHADED LIVING-ROOM	
	In a warm climate.—In a cool climate.—Warm and cold colours.	127
CHAPTER XXXV	SERVANTS' ROOMS	
	Practical and suitable attractiveness..	128
CHAPTER XXXVI	TABLE DECORATION	
	Appropriateness the keynote.—Tableware.—Linen, lace, and flowers.—Japanese simplicity.—Background.	129
CHAPTER XXXVII	WHAT TO AVOID IN INTERIOR DECORATION: RULES FOR BEGINNERS	
	Appropriateness.—Intelligent elimination.—Furnishings.—Colour scheme.—Small suites.—Background.—Placing rugs and hangings.—Treatment of long wall-space.—Men's rooms.—Table decoration.—Tea table.—How to train the taste, eye, and judgment	133

CHAPTER XXXVIII	FADS IN COLLECTING *A panier fleuri collection.—A typical experience in collecting.—A "find" in an obscure American junk-shop.—Getting on the track of some Italian pottery.—Collections used as decoration.—A "find" in Spain.*	138
CHAPTER XXXIX	WEDGWOOD POTTERY, OLD AND MODERN *The history of Wedgwood.—Josiah Wedgwood, the founder.*	144
CHAPTER XL	ITALIAN POTTERY *Statuettes.*	148
CHAPTER XLI	VENETIAN GLASS, OLD AND MODERN *Murano Museum collection.—Table-gardens in Venetian glass.*	149
IN CONCLUSION	*Four Fundamental Principles of Interior Decoration Re-stated.*	151

ILLUSTRATIONS

PLATE I	Portion of a Drawing-room, Perfect in Composition and Detail.	iii
PLATE II	Bedroom in Country House. Modern Painted Furniture.	3
PLATE III	Suggestion for Treatment of a Very Small Bedroom.	5
PLATE IV	A Man's Office in Wall Street.	8
PLATE V	A Corner of the Same Office.	12
PLATE VI	Another View of the Same Office.	15
PLATE VII	Corner of a Room, Showing Painted Furniture, Antique and Modern.	18
PLATE VIII	Example of a Perfect Mantel, Ornaments and Mirror.	24
PLATE IX	Dining-room in Country House, Showing Modern Painted Furniture.	27
PLATE X	Dining-room Furniture, Italian Renaissance, Antique.	31
PLATE XI	Corner of Dining-room in New York Apartment, Showing Section of Italian Refectory Table and Italian Chairs, both Antique and Renaissance in Style.	35
PLATE XII	An Italian Louis XVI Salon in a New York Apartment.	39
PLATE XIII	Another Side of the Same Italian Louis XVI Salon.	42
PLATE XIV	A Narrow Hall Where Effect of Width is Attained by Use of Tapestry with Vista....	45
PLATE XV	Venetian Glass, Antique and Modern........	48
PLATE XVI	Corner of a Room in a Small Empire Suite....	50
PLATE XVII	An Example of Perfect Balance and Beauty in Mantel Arrangement.	67
PLATE XVIII	Corner of a Drawing-room, Furniture Showing Directoire Influence.	71
PLATE XIX	Entrance Hall in New York Duplex Apartment. Italian Furniture.	76
PLATE XX	Combination of Studio and Living-room in New York Duplex Apartment.	79
PLATE XXI	Part of a Victorian Parlour in One of the Few Remaining New York Victorian Mansions.....	96

PLATE XXII	Two Styles of Day-beds, Modern Painted......	103
PLATE XXIII	Boudoir in New York Apartment. Painted Furniture, Antique and Reproductions.	107
PLATE XXIV	Example of Lack of Balance in Mantel Arrangement.	111
PLATE XXV	Treatment of Ground Lying Between House and Much Travelled Country Road.	114
PLATE XXVI	An Extension Roof in New York Converted into a Balcony.	117
PLATE XXVII	A Common-place Barn Made Interesting......	121
PLATE XXVIII	Narrow Entrance Hall of a New York Antique Shop.	125
PLATE XXIX	Example of a Charming Hall Spoiled by Too Pronounced a Rug.	132
PLATE XXX	A Man's Library.	136
PLATE XXXI	A Collection of Empire Furniture, Ornaments, and China.	141
PLATE XXXII	Italian Reproductions in Pottery After Classic Models.	147

"Those who duly consider the influence of the fine-arts on the human mind, will not think it a small benefit to the world, to diffuse their productions as wide, and preserve them as long as possible. The multiplying of copies of fine work, in beautiful and durable materials, must obviously have the same effect in respect to the arts as the invention of printing has upon literature and the sciences: by their means the principal productions of both kinds will be forever preserved, and will effectually prevent the return of ignorant and barbarous ages."

JOSIAH WEDGWOOD: Catalogue of 1787

One of the most joyful obligations in life should be the planning and executing of BEAUTIFUL HOMES, keeping ever in mind that distinction is not a matter of scale, since a vast palace may find its rival in the smallest group of rooms, provided the latter obeys the law of good line, correct proportions, harmonious colour scheme and appropriateness: a law insisting that all useful things be beautiful things.

CHAPTER I

HOW TO REARRANGE A ROOM

Lucky is the man or woman of taste who has no inherited eyesores which, because of association, must not be banished! When these exist in large numbers one thing only remains to be done: look them over, see to what period the majority belong, and proceed as if you *wanted* a mid-Victorian, late Colonial or brass-bedstead room.

To rearrange a room successfully, begin by taking everything out of it (in reality or in your mind), then decide how you want it to look, or how, owing to what you own and must retain, you are obliged to have it look. Design and colour of wall decorations, hangings, carpets, lighting fixtures, lamps and ornaments on mantel, depend upon the character of your furniture.

It is the mantel and its arrangement of ornaments that sound the keynote upon first entering a room.

Conventional simplicity in number and arrangement of ornaments gives balance and repose, hence dignity. Dignity once established, one can afford to be individual, and introduce a riot of colours, provided they are all in the same key. Luxurious cushions, soft rugs and a hundred and one feminine touches will create atmosphere and knit together the austere scheme of line—the anatomy of your room. Colour and textiles are the flesh of interior decoration.

In furnishing a small room you can add greatly to its apparent size by using plain paper and making the woodwork the same colour, or slightly darker in tone. If you cannot find wall paper of exactly the colour and shade you wish, it is often possible to use the wrong side of a paper and produce exactly the desired effect.

In repapering old rooms with imperfect ceilings it is easy to disguise this by using a paper with a small design in the same tone. A perfectly plain ceiling paper will show every defect in the surface of the ceiling.

If your house or flat is small you can gain a great effect of space by keeping the same colour scheme throughout—that is, the same colour or related colours. To make a small hall and each of several small rooms on the same floor different in any pronounced way, is to cut up your home into a restless, unmeaning checkerboard, where one feels conscious of the walls and all limitations. The effect of restful spaciousness may be obtained by taking the same small suite and treating its walls, floors and draperies, as has been suggested, in the same colour scheme or a scheme of related keys in colour. That is, wood browns, beiges and yellows; violets, mauves and pinks; different tones of greys; different tones of yellows, greens and blues.

Now having established your suite and hall all in one key, so that there is absolutely no jarring note as one passes from room to room, you may be sure of having achieved that most desirable of all qualities in interior decoration—repose. We have seen the idea here suggested carried out in small summer homes with most successful results; the same colour used on walls and furniture, while exactly the same chintz was employed in every bedroom, opening out of one hall. By this means it was possible to give to a small, unimportant cottage, a note of distinction otherwise quite impossible. Here, however, let us say that, if the same chintz is to be used in every room, it must be neutral in colour—a chintz in which the colour scheme is, say, yellows in different tones, browns in different tones, or greens or greys. To vary the character of each room, introduce different colours in the furniture covers, the sofa-cushions and lamp-shades. Our point is to urge the repetition of a main background in a small group of rooms; but to escape monotony by planning that the accessories in each room shall strike individual notes of decorative, contrasting colour.

PLATE II

A room with modern painted furniture is shown here. Lines and decorations Empire.

Note the lyre backs of chairs and head board in day-bed. Treatment of this bed is that suggested where twin beds are used and room affords wall space for but one of them.

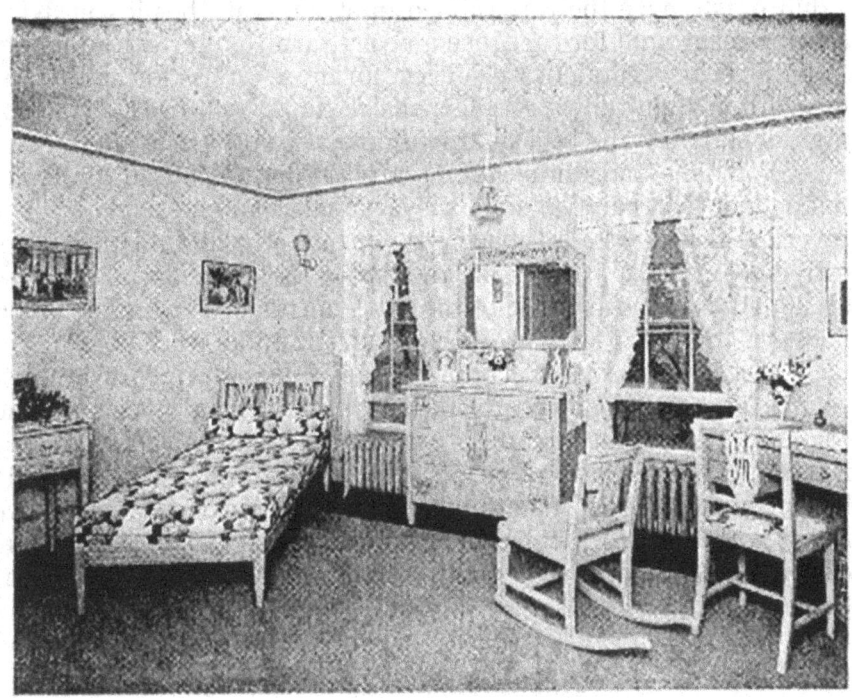

Bedroom in Country House. Modern Painted Furniture.

❖❖❖

What to do with old floors is a question many of us have faced. If your house has been built with floors of wide, common boards which have become rough and separated by age, in some cases allowing dust to sift through from the cellar, and you do not wish to go to the expense of all-over carpets, you have the choice of several methods. The simplest and least expensive is to paint or stain the floors. In this case employ a floor painter and begin by removing all old paint. Paint removers come for the purpose. Then have the floors planed to make them even. Next, fill the cracks with putty. The most practical method is to stain the floors some dark colour; mahogany, walnut, weathered oak, black, green or any colour you may prefer, and then wax them. This protects the colour. In a room where daintiness is desired, and economy is not important, as for instance in a room with white painted furniture, you may have white floors and a square carpet rug of some plain dark toned velvet; or, if preferred, the painted border may be in come delicate colour to match the wall paper. To resume, if you like a dull finish, have the wax rubbed in at intervals, but if you like a glossy background for rugs, use a heavy varnish after the floors are coloured. This treatment we suggest for more or less formal rooms. In bedrooms, put down an inexpensive filling as a background for rugs, or should yours be a summer home, use straw matting.

For halls and dining-rooms a plain dark-coloured linoleum, costing not less than two dollars a yard makes and inexpensive floor covering. If it is waxed it becomes not only very durable but, also, extremely effective, suggesting the dark tiles in Italian houses. We do not advise the purchase of the linoleums which represent inlaid floors, as they are invariably unsuccessful imitations.

If it is necessary to economise and your brass bedstead must be used even though you dislike it, you can have it painted the colour of your walls. It requires a number of coats. A soft pearl grey is good. Then use a colour, or colours, in your silk or chintz bedspread. Sun-proof material in a solid colour makes an attractive cover, with a narrow fringe in several colours straight around the edges and also, forming a circle or square on the top of the bed-cover.

***

If your gas or electric fixtures are ugly and you cannot afford more attractive ones, buy very cheap, perfectly plain, ones and paint them to match the walls, giving decorative value to them with coloured silk shades.

PLATE III

Shows one end of a very small bedroom with modern painted furniture, so simple in line and decoration that it would be equally appropriate either for a young man or for a young woman. We say "young," because there is something charmingly fresh and youthful about this type of furniture.

The colour is pale pistache green, with mulberry lines, the same combination of colours being repeated in painting the walls which have a grey background lined with mulberry—the broad stripe—and a narrow green line. The bed cover is mulberry, the lamp shade is green with mulberry and grey in the fringe.

On the walls are delightful old prints framed in black glass with gold lines, and a narrow moulding of gilded oak, an old style revived.

A square of antique silk covers the night table, and the floor is polished hard wood.

Here is your hall bedroom, the wee guest room in a flat, or the extra guest room under the eaves of your country house, made equally beguiling. The result of this artistic simplicity is a restful sense of space.

Suggestion for Treatment of a Very Small Bedroom

If you wish to use twin beds and have not wall space for them, treat one like a couch or day-bed. *See Plate II*. Your cabinet-maker can remove the footboard, then draw the bed out into the room, place in a position convenient to the light either by day or night, after which put a cover of cretonne or silk over it and cushions of the same. Never put a spotted material on a spotted material. If your couch or sofa is done in a figured material of different colours, make your sofa cushions of plain material to tone down the sofa. If the sofa is a plain colour, then tone it up—make it more decorative by using cushions of several colours.

If you like your room, but find it cold in atmosphere, try deep cream gauze for sash curtains. They are wonderful atmosphere producers. The advantage of two tiers of sash curtains (*see Plate IX*) is that one can part and push back one tier for air, light or looking out, and still use the other tier to modify the light in the room.

Another way to produce atmosphere in a cold room is to use a tone-on-tone paper. That is, a paper striped in two depths of the same colour. In choosing any wall paper it is imperative that you try a large sample of it in the room for which it is intended, as the reflection from a nearby building or brick wall can entirely change a beautiful yellow into a thick mustard colour. How a wall paper looks in the shop is no criterion. As stated sometimes the *wrong side* of wall paper gives you the tone you desire.

When rearranging your room do not desecrate the few good antiques you happen to own by the use of a too modern colour scheme. Have the necessary modern pieces you have bought to supplement your treasures stained or painted in a dull, dark colour in harmony with the antiques, and then use subdued colours in the floor coverings, curtains and cushions.

If you own no good old ornaments, try to get a few good shapes and colours in inexpensive reproductions of the desired period.

If your room is small, and the bathroom opens out of it, add to the size of the room by using the same colour scheme in the bathroom, and conceal the plumbing and fixtures by a low screen. If the connecting door is kept open, the effect is to enlarge greatly the appearance of the small bedroom, whereas if the bedroom decorations are dark and the bathroom has a light floor and walls, it abruptly cuts itself off and emphasises the smallness of the bedroom.

Everything depends upon the appropriateness of the furniture to its setting. We recall some much admired dining-room chairs in the home of the Maclaines of Lochbuie in Argyleshire, west coast of Scotland. The chairs in question are covered with sealskin from the seals caught off that rugged coast. They are quite delightful in a remote country house; but they would not be tolerated in London.

The question of placing photographs is not one to be treated lightly. Remember, intimate photographs should be placed in intimate rooms, while photographs of artists and all celebrities are appropriate for the living room or library. It is extremely seldom that a photograph unless of public interest is not out of place in a formal room.

To repeat, never forget that your house or flat is *your* home, and, that to have any charm whatever of a personal sort, it must suggest *you*—not simply the taste of a professional decorator. So work with your decorator (if you prefer to employ one) by giving your personal attention to styles and colours, and selecting those most sympathetic to your own nature. Your architect will be grateful if you will show the same interest in the details of building your home, rather than assuming the attitude that you have engaged him in order to rid yourself of such bother.

If you are building a pretentious house and decide upon some clearly defined period of architecture, let us say, Georgian (English eighteenth century) we would advise keeping your first floor mainly in that period as to furniture and hangings, but upstairs let yourself go, that is, make your rooms any style you like. Go in for a gay riot of colour, such combinations as are known as Bakst colouring,—if that happens to be your fancy. This Russian painter and designer was fortunate in having the theatre in which to demonstrate his experiments in vivid colour combinations, and sometimes we quite forget that he was but one of many who have used sunset palettes.

PLATE IV

Here we have a man's office in Wall Street, New York, showing how a lawyer with large interests surrounds himself with necessities which contribute to his comfort, sense of beauty and art instincts.

The desk is big, solid and commodious, yet artistically unusual.

A Man's Office in Wall Street

Recently the fair butterfly daughters of a mother whose taste has grown sophisticated, complained—"But, Mother, we dislike *periods*, and here you are building a Tudor house!" forgetting, by the way, that the so-called Bakst interiors, adored by them, are equally a *period*.

This home, a very wonderful one, is being worked out on the plan suggested, that is, the first floor is decorated in the period of the exterior of the house, while the personal rooms on the upper floors reflect, to a certain extent, the personality of their occupants.

Remember there must always be a certain relationship between all the rooms in one suite, the relationship indicated by lines and a background of the same, or a harmonising colour-scheme.

CHAPTER II

HOW TO CREATE A ROOM

One so often hears the complaint, "I could not possibly set out alone to furnish a room! I don't know anything about *periods*. Why, a Louis XVI chair and an Empire chair are quite the same to me. Then the question of antiques and reproductions—why any one could mislead me!"

If you have absolutely no interest in the arranging or rearranging of your rooms, house or houses, of course, leave it to a decorator and give your attention to whatever does interest you. On the other hand, as with bridge, if you really want to play the game, you can learn it. The first rule is to determine the actual use to which you intend putting the room. Is it to be a bedroom merely, or a combination of bedroom and boudoir? Is it to be a formal reception-room, or a living-room? Is it to be a family library, or a man's study? If it is a small flat, do you aim at absolute comfort, artistically achieved, or do you aim at formality at the expense of comfort?

If you lean toward both comfort and formality, and own a country house and a city abode, there will be no difficulty in solving the problem. Formality may be left to the town house or flat, while during week-ends, holidays and summers you can revel in supreme comfort.

Every man or woman is capable of creating comfort. It is a question of those deep chairs with wide seats and backs, soft springs, thick, downy cushions, of tables and bookcases conveniently placed, lights where you want them, beds to the individual taste,—double, single, or twins!

The getting together of a period room, one period or periods in combination, is difficult, especially if you are entirely ignorant of the subject. However, here is your cue. Let us suppose you need, or want, a desk—an antique desk. Go about from one dealer to the other until you find the very piece you have dreamed of; one that gives pleasure to you, as well as to the dealer. Then take an experienced friend to look at it. If you have every reason to suppose that the desk is genuine, buy it. Next, read up on the furniture of the particular period to which your desk belongs, in as serious a manner as you do when you buy a prize dog at the show. Now you have made an intelligent beginning as a collector. Reading informs you, but you must buy old furniture to be educated on that subject. Be eternally on the lookout; the really good pieces, veritable antiques, are rare; most of them are in museums, in private collections or in the hands of the most expensive dealers. I refer to those unique pieces, many of them signed by the maker and in perfect condition because during all their existence they have been jealously preserved, often by the very family and in the very house for which they were made. Our chances for picking up antiques are reduced to pieces which on account of reversed circumstances have been turned out of house and home, and, as with human wanderers, much jolting about has told upon them. Most of these are fortified in various directions, but they are treasures all the same, and have a beauty value in line colour and workmanship and a wonderful fitness for the purposes for which they were intended.

"Surely we are many men of many minds!"

PLATE V

The sofa large, strong and luxuriously comfortable; the curtains simple, durable and masculine in gender. The tapestry and architectural picture, decorative and appropriately impersonal, as the wall decorations should be in a room used merely for transacting business.

A Corner of the Same Office

Some prefer antiques a bit dilapidated; a missing detail serving as a hallmark to calm doubts; others insist upon completeness to the eye and solidity for use; while the connoisseur, with unlimited means, recognises nothing less than signed sofas and chairs, and other *objets d'art*. To repeat:—be always on the lookout, remembering that it is the man who knows the points of a good dog, horse or car who can pick a winner.

Wonderful reproductions are made in New York City and other cities, and thousands bought every day. They are beautiful and desirable pieces of furniture, ornaments or silks; but the lover of the *vrai antique* learns to detect, almost at a glance, the lack of that quality which a fine *old* piece has. It is not alone that the materials must be old. There is a certain quality gained from the long association of its parts. One knows when a piece has "found itself," as Kipling would put it. Time gives an inimitable finish to any surface.

If you are young in years, immature in taste, and limited as to bank account, you will doubtless go in for a frankly modern room, with cheerful painted furniture, gay or soft-toned chintzes, and inexpensive smart floor coverings. To begin this way and gradually to collect what you want, piece by piece, is to get the most amusement possible out of furnishing. When you have the essential pieces for any one room, you can undertake an *ensemble*. Some of the rarest collections have been got together in this way, and, if one's fortune expands instead of contracting, old pieces may be always replaced by those still more desirable, more rare, more in keeping with your original scheme.

To buy expensive furnishings in haste and without knowledge, and within a year or two discover everything to be in bad taste, is a tragedy to a person with an instinctive aversion to waste. Antique or modern, every beautiful thing bought is a cherished heirloom in embryo. Remember, we may inherit a good antique or *objet d'art*, buy one, or bequeath one. Let us never be guilty of the reverse,—a bar-sinister piece of furniture! Sympathy with unborn posterity should make us careful.

It is always excusable to retain an ugly, inartistic thing—if it is *useful*; but an ornament must be beautiful in line or in colour, or it belies its name. Practise that genuine, obvious loyalty which hides away on a safe, but invisible shelf, the bad taste of our ancestors and friends.

Having settled upon a type of furniture, turn your attention to the walls. Always let the location of your room decide the colour of its walls. The room with a sunny exposure may have any colour you like, warm or cold, but your north room or any room more or less sunless, requires the warm, sun-producing yellows, pinks, apple-greens, beige and wood-colours, never the cold colours, such as greys, mauves, violets and blues, unless in combination with the warm tones. If it is your intention to hang pictures on the walls, use plain papers. Remember you must never put a spot on a spot! The colour of your walls once established, keep in mind two things: that to be agreeable to the artistic eye your ceilings must be lighter than your sidewalls, and your floors darker. Broadly speaking, it is Nature's own arrangement, green trees and hillsides, the sky above, and the dark earth beneath our feet. A ceiling, if lighter in tone than the walls, gives a sense of airiness to a room. Floors, whether of exposed wood, completely carpeted, or covered by rugs, must be enough darker than your sidewalls to "hold down your room," as the decorators say.

If colour is to play a conspicuous part, brightly figured silks and cretonnes being used for hangings and upholstery, the floor covering should be indefinite both as to colour and design. On the other hand, when rugs or carpets are of a definite design in pronounced colours, particularly if you are arranging a living-room, make your walls, draperies and chair-covers plain, and observe great restraint in the use of colour. Those who work with them know that there is no such thing as an ugly colour, for all colours are beautiful. Whether a colour makes a beautiful or an ugly effect depends entirely upon its juxtaposition to other tones. How well French milliners and dressmakers understand this! To make the point quite clear, let us take magenta. Used alone, nothing has more style, more beautiful distinction, but in wrong combination magenta can be amazingly, depressingly ugly. Magenta with blue is ravishing, beautiful in the subtle way old tapestries are: it touches the imagination whenever that combination is found.

PLATE VI

The table is modern, but made on the lines of a refectory table, well suited in length, width and solidity for board meetings, etc.

The chairs are Italian in style.

Another View of the Same Office

We grow up to, into, and out of colour schemes. Each of the Seven Ages of Man has its appropriate setting in colour as in line. One learns the dexterous manipulation of colour from furnishing, as an artist learns from painting.

Refuse to accept a colour scheme, unless it appeals to your individual taste—no matter who suggests it. To one not very sensitive to colour here is a valuable suggestion. Find a bit of beautiful old silk brocade, or a cretonne you especially like, and use its colour combinations for your room—a usual device of decorators.

Let us suppose your silk or cretonne to have a deep-cream background, and scattered on it green foliage, faded salmon-pink roses and little, fine blue flowers. Use its prevailing colour, the deep cream, for walls and possibly woodwork; make the draperies of taffeta or rep in soft apple-greens; use the same colour for upholstery, make shades for lamp and electric lights of salmon-pink, then bring in a touch of blue in a sofa cushion, a footstool or small chair, or in a beautiful vase which charms by its shape as well by reproducing the exact tone of blue you desire. There are some who insist no room is complete without its note of blue. Many a room has been built up around some highly prized treasure,—lovely vase or an old Japanese print.

A thing always to be avoided is monotony in colour. Who can not recall barren rooms, without a spark of attraction despite priceless treasures, dispersed in a meaningless way? That sort of setting puts a blight on any gathering. "Well," you will ask, "given the task of converting such a sterile stretch of monotony into a blooming joy, how should one begin?" It is quite simple. Picture to yourself how the room would look if you scattered flowers about it, roses, tulips, mignonette, flowers of yellow and blue, in the pell-mell confusion of a blooming garden. Now imitate the flower colours by *objets d'art* so judiciously placed that in a trice you will admire what you once found cold. As if by magic, a white, cream, beige or grey room may be transformed into a smiling bower, teeming with personality, a room where wit and wisdom are spontaneously let loose.

If your taste be for chintzes and figured silks, take it as a safe rule, that given a material with a light background, it should be the same in tone as your walls; the idea being that by this method you get the full decorative value of the pattern on chintz or silk.

Figured materials can increase or diminish the size of a room, open up vistas, push back your walls, or block the vision. For this reason it is unsafe to buy material before trying the effect of it in its destined abode.

Remember that the matter of *background* is of the greatest importance when arranging your furniture and ornaments. See that your piano is so placed that the pianist has an unbroken background, of wall, tapestry, a large piece of rare old sills, or a mirror. Clyde Fitch, past-master at interior decoration, placed his piano in front of broad windows, across which at night were drawn crimson damask curtains. Some of us will never forget Geraldine Farrar, as she sat against that background wearing a dull, clinging blue-green gown, going over the score,—from memory,—of "Salomé."

The aim is to make the performer at the piano the object of interest, therefore place no diverting objects, such as pictures or ornaments, on a line with the listener's eye, except as a vague background.

There can be no more becoming setting for a group of people dining by candle or electric light, than walls panelled with dark wood to the ceiling, or a high wainscoting.

A beautiful sitting-room, not to be forgotten, had light violet walls, dull-gold frames on the furniture which was covered in deep-cream brocades, bits of old purple velvets and violet silks on the tables, under large bowls of Benares bronze filled with violets. The grand piano was protected by a piece of old brocade in faded yellows, and our hostess, a well-known singer, usually wore a simple Florentine tea-gown of soft violet velvet, which together with the lighter violet walls, set off her fair skin and black hair to beautiful advantage.

Put a figured, many-coloured sofa cushion behind the head of a pretty woman, and if the dominating colour is becoming to her, she is still pretty, but change it to a solid black, purple or dull-gold and see how instantly the degree of her beauty is enhanced by being thrown into relief.

PLATE VII

Gives attractive corner by a window, the heavy silk brocade curtains of which are drawn. A standard electric lamp lights the desk, both modern-painted pieces, and the beautiful old flower picture, black background with a profusion of colours in lovely soft tones, is framed by a dull-gold moulding and gives immense distinction. The chair is Venetian Louis XV, the same period as desk in style.

Not to be ignored in this picture is a tin scrap basket beautifully proportioned and painted a vivid emerald green; a valuable addition a note of cheerful colour. The desk and wooden standard of lamp are painted a deep blue-plum colour, touched with gold, and the silk curtains are soft mulberry, in two tones.

Corner of Room, Showing Painted Furniture, Antique and Modern

Study values—just why and how much any decorative article decorates, and remember in furnishing a room, decorating a wall or dining-room table, it is not the intrinsic value or individual beauty of any one article which counts. Each picture on the wall, each piece of furniture, each bit of silver, glass, china, linen or lace, each yard of chintz or silk, every carpet or rug must be beautiful and effective *in relation to the others used*, for the *art* of interior decoration lies in this subtle, or obvious, relationship of furnishings.

We acknowledge as legitimate all schemes of interior decoration and insist that what makes any scheme good or bad, successful, or unsuccessful presuming a knowledge of the fundamentals of the art, is the fact that it is planned in reference to the type of man or woman who is to live in it.

A new note has been struck of late in the arranging of bizarre, delightful rooms which on entering we pronounce "very amusing."

Original they certainly are, in colour combinations, tropical in the impression they make,—or should we say Oriental?

They have come to us via Russia, Bakst, Munich and Martine of Paris. Like Rheinhardt's staging of "Sumurun," because these blazing interiors strike us at an unaccustomed angle, some are merely astonished, others charmed as well. There are temperaments ideally set in these interiors, and there are houses where they are in place. We cannot regard them as epoch-making, but granted that there is no attempt to conform to two of the rules for furnishing,— *appropriateness* and *practicality*, the results are refreshingly new and entertaining. This is one of the instances where exaggeration has served as a healthy antidote to the tendency toward extreme dinginess rampant about ten years ago, resulting from an obsession to antique everything. The reaction from this, a flaming rainbow of colours, struck a blow to the artistic sense, drew attention back to the value of colour and started the creative impulse along the line of a happy medium.

Whether it be a furnished porch, personal suite (as bedroom, boudoir and bath), a family living-room, dining-room, formal reception-room, or period ballroom, never allow members of your household or servants to destroy the effect you have achieved with careful thought and outlay of money, by ruthlessly moving chairs and tables from one room to another. Keep your wicker furniture on the porch, for which it was intended. If it strays into the adjacent living-room, done in quite another scheme, it will absolutely thwart your efforts at harmony, while your porch-room done in wicker and gay chintzes, striped awnings and geranium rail-boxes, cries out against the intrusion of a chair dragged out from the house.

Remember that should you intend using your period ballroom from time to time as an audience room for concerts and lectures, you must provide a complete equipment of small, very light (so as to be quickly moved) chairs, in your "period," as a necessary part of your decoration.

The current idea that a distinguished room remains distinguished because costly tapestries and old masters hang on its walls, even when the floor is strewn with vulgar, hired chairs, is an absurd mistake. Each room from kitchen to ballroom is a stage "set,"—a harmonious background for certain scenes in life's drama. It is the man or woman who grasps this principle of a distinguished home who can create an interior which endures, one which will hold its own despite the ebb and flow of fashion. Imposing dimensions and great outlay of money do not necessarily imply distinction, a quality depending upon unerring good taste in the minutest details, one which may be achieved equally in a stately mansion, in a city flat, or in a cottage by the sea.

The question of background is absorbingly interesting. A vase, with or without flowers, to add to the composition of your room, that is, to make "a good picture," must be placed so that its background sets it off. Let the Venetian glass vase holding one rose stand in such a position that your green curtain is its background, and not a photograph or other picture. One flower, carefully placed in a room, will have more real decorative value than dozens of costly roses strewn about in the wrong vases, against mottled, line-destroying backgrounds.

Flowers are always more beautiful in a plain vase, whether of glass, pottery, porcelain or silver. If a vase chances to have a decoration in colour, then make a point of having the flowers it holds accord in colour, if not in shade, with the colour or colours in the vase.

There is a general rule that no ornament should ever be placed in front of a picture. The exception to this rule occurs when the picture is one of the large, architectural variety, whose purpose is primarily mural decoration,—an intentional background, as tapestries often are, serving its purpose as nature does when a vase or statue is placed in a park or garden. One sees in portraits by some of the old masters this idea of landscape used as background. Bear in mind, however, that if there is a central design—a definite composition in the picture, or tapestry, no ornament should ever be so placed as to interfere with it. If you happen to own a tapestry which is not large enough for your space by one, two or three feet, frame it with a plain border of velvet or velveteen, to match the dominating colour, and a shade darker than it appears in the tapestry. This expedient heightens the decorative effect of the tapestry.

CHAPTER III

HOW TO DETERMINE CHARACTER OF HANGINGS AND FURNITURE-COVERING FOR A GIVEN ROOM

In a measure, the materials for hangings and furniture-coverings are determined more or less by the amount one wishes to spend in this direction. For choice, one would say silk or velvet for formal rooms; velvets, corduroys or chintz for living-rooms; leather and corduroy with rep hangings for a man's study or smoking-room; thin silks and chintz for bedrooms; chintz for nurseries, breakfast-rooms and porches.

In England, slip-covers of chintz (glazed cretonne) appear, also, in formal rooms; but are removed when the owner is entertaining. If the permanent upholstery is of chintz, then at once your room becomes informal. If you are planning the living-room for a small house or apartment, which must serve as reception-room during the winter months, far more dignity, and some elegance can be obtained for the same expenditure, by using plain velveteen, modern silk brocades in one colour, or some of the modern reps to be had in very smart shades of all colours.

If your furniture is choice, rarely beautiful in quality, line and colour, hangings and covers must accord. Genuine antiques demand antique silks for hangings and table covers; but no decorator, if at all practical, will cover a chair or sofa in the frail old silks, for they go to pieces almost in the mounting. Waive sentiment in this case, for the modern reproductions are satisfactory to the eye and improve in tone with age.

If you own only a small piece of antique silk, make a square of it for the centre of the table, or cleverly combine several small bits, if these are all you have, into an interesting cover or cushion. Nothing in the world gives such a note of distinction to a room as the use of rare, old silks, properly placed.

The fashion for cretonne and chintz has led to their indiscriminate use by professionals as well as amateurs, and this craze has caused a prejudice against them. Chintz used with judgment can be most attractive. In America the term chintz includes cretonne and stamped linen. If you are planning for them, put together, for consideration, all your bright coloured chintz, and in quite another part of your room, or decorator's shop, the chintz of dull, faded colours, as they require different treatment. A general rule for this material—bright or dull—is that if you would have your chintz *decorate*, be careful not to use it too lavishly. If it is intended for curtains, then cover only one chair with it and cover the rest in a solid colour. If you want chintz for all of your chairs and sofa, make your curtains, sofa cushions and lamp shades of a solid colour, and be sure that you take one of the leading colours in the chintz. Next indicate your intention at harmony, by "bringing together" the plain curtains or chairs, and your chintz, with a narrow fringe or border of still another colour, which figures in the chintz. Let us suppose chintz to be black with a design in greens, mulberry and buff. Make your curtains plain mulberry, edged with narrow pale green fringe with black and buff in it, or should your chintz be grey with a design in faded blues and violets and a touch of black, make curtains of the chintz, and cover one large chair, keeping the sofa and the remaining chairs grey, with the bordering fringe, or gimp, in one or two of the other shades, sofa cushions and the lamp shades in blues and violets (lining lamp shades with thin pink silk), and use a little black in the bordering fringe.

PLATE VIII

Shows an ideal mantel arrangement, faultless as a composition and beautiful and rare in detail. The exquisite white marble mantel is Italian, not French, of the time of Louis XVI.

Though the designs of this period are almost identical, one quickly learns to detect the difference in feeling between the work of the two countries. The Italians are freer, broader in their treatment, show more movement and in a way more grace, where the French work is more detailed and precise, hence at times, by contrast, seems stilted and rigid.

Enchantingly graceful are the two candelabra, also Louis XVI, while the central ornament is ideally chosen for size and design.

The dull gold frame of the mirror is very beautiful, and the painting above the glass interesting and unusual as to subject and execution.

The chair is a good example of Italian Louis XV.

Example of a Perfect Mantel, Ornaments and Mirror

If you decide upon a very brilliant chintz use it only in one chair, a screen, or in a valance over plain curtains with straps to hold them back, or perhaps a sofa cushion. Whether a chintz is bright or dull, its pattern is important. As with silks, brocaded in different colours, therefore never use chintz where a chair or sofa calls for tufting. A tufted piece of furniture always looks best done in plain materials.

In using a chintz in which both colour and design are indefinite, the kind which gives more or less an impression of faded tapestry, you will find that the very indefiniteness of the pattern makes it possible to use the chintz with more freedom, being always sure of a harmonious background. The one thing to guard against is that on entering a room you must not be conscious either of several colours, or of any set design.

CHAPTER IV

THE STORY OF TEXTILES

The story of the evolution of textiles (any woven material) is fascinating, and like the history of every art, runs parallel with the history of culture and progress in the art of living,—physical, mental and spiritual.

To those who feel they would enjoy an exhaustive history of textiles we recommend a descriptive catalogue relating to the collection of textiles in the South Kensington Museum, prepared by the Very Rev. Daniel Rock, D.D. (1870).

In the introduction to that catalogue one gets the story of woven linens, cottons, silks, paper, gold and silver threads, interspersed with precious jewels and glass beads—all materials woven by hand or machine.

The story of textiles includes: 1st, woven materials; 2nd, embroidered materials; 3rd, a combination of the two, known as "tapestry." If one reads their wonderful story, starting in Assyria, then progressing to Egypt, the Orient, Greece, Rome and Western Europe, in any history of textiles, one may obtain quickly and easily a clear idea of this department of interior decoration from the very earliest times.

The first European silk is said to have been in the form of transparent gauze, dyed lovely tones for women of the Greek islands, a form of costume later condemned by Greek philosophers.

We know that embroidery was an art three thousand years ago, in fact the figured garments seen on the Assyrian and Egyptian bas-reliefs are supposed to represent materials with embroidered figures—not woven patterns—whereas in the Bible, when we read of embroidery, according to the translators, this sometimes means woven stripes.

PLATE IX

An ideal dining-room of its kind, modern painted furniture, Empire in design. In this case yellow with decoration in white. Curtains, thin yellow silk.

Note the Empire electric light fixtures in hand-carved gilded wood, reproductions of an antique silver applique. Even the steam radiators are here cleverly concealed by wooden cases made after Empire designs.

The walls are white and panelled in wood also white.

Dining-room in Country House, Showing Modern Painted Furniture. Style Directoire.

The earliest garments of Egypt were of cotton and hemp, or mallow, resembling flax. The older Egyptians never knew silks in any form, nor did the Israelites, nor any of the ancients. The earliest account of this material is given by Aristotle (fourth century). It was brought into Western Europe from China, via India, the Red Sea and Persia, and the first to weave it outside the Orient was a maiden on the Isle of Cos, off the coast of Asia Minor, producing a thin gauze-like tissue worn by herself and companions, the material resembling the Seven Veils of Salome. To-day those tiny bits of gauze one sees laid in between the leaves of old manuscript to protect the illuminations, as our publishers use sheets of tissue paper, are said to be examples of this earliest form of woven silk.

The Romans used silk at first only for their women, as it was considered not a masculine material, but gradually they adopted it for the festival robes of men, Titus and Vespasian being among those said to have worn it.

The first silk looms were set up in the royal palaces of the Roman kings in the year 533 A.D. The raw material was brought from the East for a long time but in the sixth century two Greek monks, while in China, studied the method of rearing silk worms and obtaining the silk, and on their departure are said to have concealed the eggs of silk worms in their staves. They are accredited with introducing the manufacture of silk into Greece and hence into Western Europe. After that Greece, Persia and Asia Minor made this material, and Byzantium was famed for its silks, the actual making of which got into the hands of the Jews and was for a long time controlled by them.

Metals (gold, silver and copper) were flattened out and cut into narrow strips for winding around cotton twists. These were the gold and silver threads used in weaving. The Moors and Spaniards instead of metals used strips of gilded parchment for weaving with the silk.

We know that England was weaving silk in the thirteenth century, and velvets seem to have been used at a very early date. The introduction of silk and velvet into different countries had an immediate and much-needed influence in civilising the manners of society. It is hard to realise that in the thirteenth century when Edward I married Eleanor of Castile, the highest nobles of England when resting at their ease, stretched at full length on the straw-covered floors of baronial halls, and jeered at the Spanish courtiers who hung the walls and stretched the floors of Edward's castle with silks in preparation for his Spanish bride.

The progress of art and culture was always from the East and moved slowly. Do not go so far back as the thirteenth century. James I of England owned no stockings when he was James VI of Scotland, and had to borrow a pair in which to receive the English ambassador.

In the eleventh century Italy manufactured her own silks, and into them were woven precious stones, corals, seed pearls and coloured glass beads which were made in Greece and Venice, as well as gold and silver spangles (twelfth and thirteenth centuries).

Here is an item on interior decorations from Proverbs vii, 16; "I have woven my bed with cords, I have covered it with painted tapestry brought from Egypt." There were painted tapestries made in Western Europe at a very early date, and collectors eagerly seek them (*see Plate XIV*). In the fourteenth century these painted tapestries were referred to as "Stained Cloth."

Embroidery as an art, as we have already seen, antedates silk weaving. The youngest of the three arts is tapestry. The oldest embroidery stitches are: "the feather stitch," so called because they all took one direction, the stitches over-lapping, like the feathers of a bird; and "cross-stitch" or "cushion" style, because used on church cushions, made for kneeling when at prayer or to hold the Mass book.

Hand-woven tapestries are called "comb-wrought" because the instrument used in weaving was comb-like.

"Cut-work" is embroidery that is cut out and appliqued, or sewed on another material.

Carpets which were used in Western Europe in the Middle Ages are seldom seen. The Kensington Museum owns two specimens, both of them Spanish, one of the fourteenth and one of the fifteenth century.

In speaking of Gothic art we called attention to the fostering of art by the Church during the Dark Ages. This continued, and we find that in Henry VIII's time those who visited monasteries and afterward wrote accounts of them call attention to the fact that each monk was occupied either with painting, carving, modelling, embroidering or writing. They worked primarily for the Church, decorating it for the glory of God, but the homes of the rich and powerful laity, even so early as the reign of Henry III (1216-1272), boasted some very beautiful interior decorations, tapestries, painted ceilings and stained glass, as well as carved panelling.

Bostwick Castle, Scotland, had its vaulted ceiling painted with towers, battlements and pinnacles, a style of mural decoration which one sees in the oldest castles of Germany. It recalls the illumination in old manuscripts.

CHAPTER V

CANDLESTICKS, LAMPS, FIXTURES FOR GAS AND ELECTRICITY, AND SHADES

Candlesticks, lamps, and fixtures for gas and electricity must accord with the lines of your architecture and furniture. The mantelpiece is the connecting link between the architecture and the furnishing of a room. It is the architect's contribution to the furnishing, and for this reason the keynote for the decorator.

In the same way lighting fixtures are links between the construction and decoration of a room, and can contribute to, or seriously divert from, the decorator's design.

It is important that fixtures be so placed as to appear a part of the decoration and not merely to illuminate conveniently a corner of the room, a writing-desk, table or piano.

PLATE X

The dining-room of this apartment is Italian Renaissance—oak, almost black from age, and carved.

The seat pads and lambrequin over window are of deep red velvet. The walls are stretched with dull red *brocotello* (a combination of silk and linen), very old and valuable. The chandelier is Italian carved wood, gilded.

Attention is called to the treatment of the windows. No curtains are used, instead, boxes are planted with ivy which is trained to climb the green lattice and helps to temper the light, while the window shades themselves are of a fascinating glazed linen, having a soft yellow background and design of fruit and vines in brilliant colours.

Dining-room Furniture, Italian Renaissance

In planning your house after arranging for proper wall space for your various articles of furniture, keep in mind always that lights will be needed and must be at the same time conveniently placed and distinctly decorative.

One is astonished to see how often the actual balance of a room is upset by the careless placing of electric fixtures. Therefore keep in mind when deciding upon the lighting of a room the following points: first, fixtures must follow in line style of architecture and furniture; second, the position of fixtures on walls must carry out the architect's scheme of proportion, line and balance; third, the material used in fixtures—brass, gilded wood, glass or wrought iron—must contribute to the decorator's scheme of line and colour; fourth, as a contribution to colour scheme the fixtures must be in harmony with the colour of the side walls, so as not to cut them up, and the shade should be a *light* note of colour, not one of the *dark* notes when illuminated.

This brings us to the question of shades. The selecting of shapes and colours for shading the lights in your rooms is of the greatest importance, for the shades are one of the harmonics for striking important colour notes, and their value must be equal by day and by night; that is, equally great, *even if different*. Some shades, beautiful and decorative by daylight, when illuminated, lose their colour and become meaningless blots in a room. We have in mind a large silk lamp shade of faded sage green, mauve, faun and a dull blue, the same combination appearing in the fringe—a combination not only beautiful, but harmonising perfectly with the old Gothic tapestry on the nearby wall. Nothing could be more decorative in this particular room during the day than the shade described; but were it not for the shell-pink lining, gleaming through the silk of the shade when lighted, it would have no decorative value at all at night.

In ordering or making shades, be sure that you select colours and materials which produce a diffused light. A soft thin pink silk as a lining for a silk or cretonne shade is always successful, and if a delicate pink, never clashes with the colours on the outside. A white silk lining is cold and unbecoming. A dark shade unlined, or a light coloured shade unlined, even if pink, unless the silk is shirred very full, will not give a diffused, yellow light.

It is because Italian parchment-paper produces the desired *glow* of light that it has become so popular for making shades, and, coming as it does in deep soft cream, it gives a lovely background for decorations which in line and colour can carry out the style of your room.

Figured Italian papers are equally popular for shades, but their characteristic is to decorate the room by daylight only, and to impart no *quality* to the light which they shade. Unless in pale colours, they stop the light, absolutely, throwing it down, if on a lamp, and back against the wall, if on side brackets. Therefore decorators now cut out the lovely designs on these figured papers and use them as appliques on a deep cream parchment background.

When you decide upon the shape of your shades do not forget that successful results depend upon absolutely correct proportions. Almost any shape, if well proportioned as to height and width, can be made beautiful, and the variety and effect desired, may be secured by varying the colours, the design of decoration, if any, or the texture or the length of fringe.

The "umbrella" shades with long chiffon curtains reaching to the table, not unlike a woman's hat with loose-hanging veil, make a charming and practical lamp shade for a boudoir or a woman's summer sitting-room, especially if furnished in lacquer or wicker. It is a light to rest or talk by, not for reading nor writing.

The greatest care is required in selecting shades for side-wall lights, because they quickly catch the eye upon entering a room and materially contribute to its appearance or detract from it.

CHAPTER VI

WINDOW SHADES AND AWNINGS

The first thing to consider in selecting window shades when furnishing a *house*, is whether their colour harmonises with the exterior. Keeping this point in mind, further limit your selection to those colours and tones which harmonise with your colour schemes for the interior. If you use white net or scrim, your shades must be white, and if ecru net, your shades must be ecru. If the outside of your house calls for one colour in shades and the interior calls for another, use two sets. Your dark-green sun shades never interfere, as they can always be covered by the inner set. Sometimes the dark green harmonises with the colouring of the rooms.

A room often needs, for sake of balance, to be weighted by colour on the window sides more than your heavy curtains (silk or cretonne) contribute when drawn back; in such a case decorators use coloured gauze for sash curtains in one, two or three shades and layers, which are so filmy and delicate both in texture and colouring that they allow air and light to pass through them, the effect being charming.

Another way to obtain the required colour value at your windows is the revival of glazed linens, with beautiful coloured designs, made up into shades. These are very attractive in a sunny room where the strong light brings out the design of flowers, fruits or foliage. *Plate X* shows a room in which this style of shade is used with great success. It is to be especially commended in such a case as *Plate X*, where no curtains are used at windows. Here the figured linen shade is a deliberate contribution to the decorative scheme of the room and completes it as no other material could.

Awnings can make or mar a house, give it style or keep it in the class of the commonplace. So choose carefully with reference to the colour of your house. The fact that awnings show up at a great distance and never "in the hand," as it were, argues in favour of clear stripes, in two colours and of even size, with as few extra threads of other colours as possible.

PLATE XI

Shows a part of a fine, old Italian refectory table, and one of the chairs, also antiques, which are beautifully proportioned and made comfortable with cushions of dark red velvet, in colour like curtains at window, which are of silk brocade.

The standard electric lamps throw the light *up* only. There are four, one in each corner of the room, and candles light the table.

The wall decoration here is a flower picture.

Corner of Dining-room in New York Apartment, Showing Section of Italian Refectory Table and Italian Chairs, Both Antique and Renaissance

All awnings fade, even in one season; green is, perhaps, the least durable in the sun, yellows and browns look well the longest. Fortunately an awning, a discouraging sight when taken down and in a collapsed mass of faded canvas, will often look well when up and stretched, because the strong light brings out the fresh colour of the inside. Hence one finds these rather expensive necessities of summer homes may be used for several seasons.

CHAPTER VII

TREATMENT OF PICTURES AND PICTURE FRAMES

Strive to have the subject of your pictures appropriate to the room in which they are to be hung.

It is impossible to state a rule for this, however, because while there are many styles of pictures which all are able to classify, such as old paintings which are antique in colouring, method and subject, portraits, figure pictures, architectural pictures, flower and fruit pictures, modern oil paintings of various subjects (modern in subject, method and colouring), water colours, etchings, sporting prints, fashion prints, etc., there is, also, a subtle relationship between them seen and felt only by the connoisseur, which leads him to hang in the same room, portraits, architectural pictures and flower pictures, with beautiful and successful results. Often the relationship hangs on similarity in period, style of painting or colour scheme. Your expert will see decorative value in a painting which has no individual beauty nor intrinsic worth when taken out of a particular setting.

The selecting of pictures for a room hinges first on their decorative value. That is, their colour and size, and whether the subjects are appropriate and sympathetic.

Always avoid heavy gold frames on paintings, for, unless they are real objects of art, one gets far more distinction by using a narrow black moulding. When in doubt always err on the side of simplicity.

If your object is economy as well as simplicity, and you are by chance just beginning to furnish your house and own no pictures, we would suggest good photographs of your favourite old masters, framed close, without a margin, in the passepartout method (glass with a narrow black paper tape binding).

Old coloured prints need narrow black passepartout, while broad passepartout in pink, blue or pale green to match the leading tone in wall paper makes your quaint, old black-and-white prints very decorative.

Never use white margins on any pictures unless your walls are white.

The decorative value of any picture when hung, is dependent upon its background, the height at which it is hung, its position with regard to the light, its juxtaposition to other pictures, and the character of those other pictures—that is, their subjects, colour and line.

If you are buying pictures to hang in a picture gallery, there is nothing to consider beyond the attraction of the individual picture in mind. But if you are buying a picture to hang on the walls of a room which you are furnishing, you have first to consider it as pure *decoration*; that is, to ask yourself if in colour, period and subject it carries out the idea of your room.

A modern picture is usually out of place in a room furnished with antiques. In the same way a strictly modern room is not a good setting for an old picture, if toned by time.

If you own or would own a modern portrait or landscape and it is the work of an artist, and beautiful in colour, why not "star" it,—build your room up to it? If you decide to do this, see that everything else representing *colour* is either subservient to the picture, or if of equal value as to colour, that they harmonise perfectly with the picture in mind.

PLATE XII

From a studio one enters a smaller room, one side of which is shown here, a veritable Italian Louis XVI salon.

An Italian Louis XVI Salon in a New York Apartment

We were recently shown a painting giving a view of Central Park from the Plaza Hotel, New York, under a heavy fall of snow, in the late afternoon, when the daylight still lingered, although the electric lights had begun to spangle the scene. The prevailing tone was a delicate, opalescent white, shading from blue to mauve, and we were told that one of our leading decorators intended to hang it in a blue room which he was furnishing for a New York client.

Etchings are at their best with other etchings, engravings or water colours, and should be hung in rooms flooded with light and delicately furnished.

The crowding of walls with pictures is always bad; hang only as many as *furnish* the walls, and have these on a line with the eye and when the pictures vary but slightly in size make a point of having either the tops of the frames or the bottoms on the same line,—that is, an equal distance from floor or ceiling. If this rule is observed a sense of order and restfulness is communicated to the observer.

If one picture is hung over the other uniformity and balance must be preserved.

One large picture may be balanced by two smaller ones.

Hang your miniatures in a straight line across your wall, under a large picture or in a straight line—one under the other, down a narrow wall panel.

CHAPTER VIII

TREATMENT OF PIANO CASES

A professional pianist invariably prefers the case of his or her piano left in its simple ebony or mahogany, and would not approve of its being relegated to the furniture department and decorated accordingly, any more than your violinist, or harpist, would hand over his violin, or harp, for decoration.

When a piano, however, is not the centre of interest in a house, and the artistic ensemble of decorative line and colour is, the piano case is often ordered at the piano factory to be made to accord in line with the period of the room for which it is intended, after which it is decorated so as to harmonise with the colours in the room. This can be done through the piano factory; but in the case of redecorating a room, one can easily get some independent artist to do this work, a man who has made a study of the decorations on old spinets in palaces, private mansions and museums. Some artists have been very successful in converting what was an inartistic piece of furniture as to size, outline and colour, into an object which became a pleasing portion of the colour scheme because in proper relation to the whole.

You can always make an ebony or mahogany piano case more in harmony with its setting by covering it, when not in use, with a piece of beautiful old brocade, or a modern reproduction.

PLATE XIII

Another side of same Italian Louis XVI salon. The tea-table is a modern painted convenience, the two vases are Italian pharmacy jars and the standard for electric lights is a modern-painted piece.

Another Side of Same Italian Louis XVI Salon

CHAPTER IX

TREATMENT OF DINING-ROOM BUFFETS AND DRESSING-TABLES

A dining-room buffet requires the same dignity of treatment demanded by a mantelpiece whether the silver articles kept on it be of great or small intrinsic value. Here, as in every case, appropriateness dictates the variety of articles, and the observance of the rule that there shall be no crowding nor disorder in the placing of articles insures that they contribute decorative value; in a word, the size of your buffet limits the amount of silver, glass, etc., to be placed upon it.

The variety and number of articles on a dressing-table are subject to the same two laws: that is, every article must be useful and in line and colour accord with the deliberate scheme of your room, and there must be no crowding nor disorder, no matter how rare or beautiful the toilet articles are.

CHAPTER X

TREATMENT OF WORK TABLES, BIRD CAGES, DOG BASKETS AND FISH GLOBES

Every bedroom planned for a woman, young or old, calls for a work table, work basket or work bag, or all three, and these furnish opportunities for additional "flowers" in your room; for we insist upon regarding accessories as opportunities for extra colour notes which harmonise with the main colour scheme and enliven your interior quite as flowers would, cheering it up—and, incidentally, its inmates! Apropos of this, it was only the other day that some one remarked in our hearing, "This room is so blooming with lovely bits of colour in lamp shades, pillows, and *objets d'art*, that I no longer spend money on cut flowers." There we have it! Precisely the idea we are trying to express. So make your work-table, if you own the sort with a silk work-bag suspended from the lower part, your work-basket or work-bag, represent one, two or three of the colours in your room.

If some one gives you an inharmonious work-bag, either build a room up to it, or give it away, but never hang it out in a room done in an altogether different colour scheme.

Bird-cages, dog-baskets and fish-globes may become harmonious instead of jarring colour notes, if one will give a little thought to the matter. In fact some of the black iron wrought cages when occupied by a wonderful parrot with feathers of blue and orange, red and grey, or red, blue and yellow, can be the making of certain rooms. And there are canaries with deep orange feathers which look most decorative in cages painted dark green, as well as the many-coloured paroquet, lovely behind golden bars.

Many a woman when selecting a dog has bought one which harmonised with her costume, or got a costume to set off her dog! Certainly a dark or light brindle bull is a perfect addition to a room done in browns, as is a red Chow or a tortoise-shell cat.

See to it that cage and basket set off your bird, dog or cat; but don't let them become too conspicuous notes of colour in your room or on your porch; let it be the bird, the dog or the cat which has a colour value.

The fish-globe can be of white or any colour glass you prefer, and your fish vivid or pale in tone; whichever it is, be sure that they furnish a needed—not a superfluous—tone of colour in a room or on a porch.

PLATE XIV

Shows narrow hall in an old country house, thought impossible as to appearance, but made charming by "pushing out" the wall with an antique painted tapestry and keeping all woodwork and carpets the same delicate dove grey.

A Narrow Hall Where Effect of Width Is Attained by Use of Tapestry with Vista

CHAPTER XI

TREATMENT OF FIREPLACES

Nothing is ever more attractive than the big open fireplace, piled with blazing logs, and with fire-dogs or andirons of brass or black iron, as may accord with the character of your room. If yours is a *period* room it is possible to get andirons to match, veritable old ones, by paying for them. The attractiveness of a fireplace depends largely upon its proportions. To look well it should always be wider than high, and deep enough to insure that the smoke goes up the chimney, and not out into your room. If your fireplace smokes you may need a special flue, leading from fireplace to proper chimney top, or a brass hood put on front of the fireplace.

Many otherwise attractive fireplaces are spoiled by using the wrong kind of tiles to frame them. Shiny, enamelled tiles in any colour, are bad, and pressed red brick of the usual sort equally bad, so if you are planning the fireplace of an informal room, choose tiles with a dull finish or brick with a simple rough finish. In period rooms often beautiful light or heavy mouldings entirely frame the three sides of the fireplace when it is of wood. *Well designed* marble mantels are always desirable. This feature of decoration is distinctly within the province of your architect, one reason more why he and the interior decorator, whether professional or amateur, should continually confer while building or rebuilding a house.

For coal fires we have a variety of low, broad grates; as well as reproductions of Colonial grates, which are small and swung high between brass uprights, framing the fireplace, with an ash drawer, the front of which is brass. If you prefer the *old*, one can find this variety of grate in antique shops as well as "Franklin stoves" (portable open fireplaces).

If your rooms are heated with steam, cover the radiators with wooden frames in line with the period of your room cut in open designs to allow heat to come through, and painted to match the woodwork of the room. See _Plate XIX_.

Let the fireplace be the centre of attraction in your room and draw about it comfortable chairs, sofas and settles,—make it easy to enjoy its hospitable blaze.

CHAPTER XII

TREATMENT OF BATHROOMS

Sumptuous bathrooms are not modern inventions, on the contrary the bath was a religion with the ancient Greeks, and a luxury to the early Italians. What we have to say here is in regard to the bath as a necessity for all classes.

The treatment of bathrooms has become an interesting branch of interior decoration, whereas once it was left entirely to the architect and plumber.

First, one has to decide whether the bathroom is to be finished in conventional white enamel, which cannot be surpassed for dainty appearance and sanitary cleanliness. Equally dainty to look at and offering the same degree of sanitary cleanliness, is a bathroom enamelled in some delicate tone to accord in colour with the bedroom with which it connects.

PLATE XV

This illustration speaks for itself—fruit dishes and fruit, candlesticks, covered jars for dried rose leaves, finger bowls, powder boxes, flower vase, and scent bottles—all of Venetian Glass in exquisite shades.

Venetian Glass, Antique and Modern

Some go so far as to make the bathroom the same colour as the bedroom, even when this is dark. We have in mind a bath opening out of a man's bedroom. The bedroom is decorated in dull blues, taupe and mulberry. The bathroom has the walls painted in broad stripes of dull blue and taupe, the stripes being quite six inches wide. The floor is tiled in large squares of the same blue and taupe; the tub and other furnishings are in dull blue enamel, and the wall-cabinets (one for shaving brushes, tooth brushes, etc., another for shaving cups, medicine glasses, drinking glasses, etc., and the third for medicines, soaps, etc.) are painted a dull mulberry. Built into the front of each cabinet door is an old coloured print covered with glass and framed with dull blue moulding and on the inside of each cabinet door is a mirror. One small closet in the bathroom is large enough to hang bath robe, pajamas, etc., while another is arranged for drying towels and holds a soiled clothes basket. On the inside of both doors are full-length mirrors.

The criticism that mirrors in men's bathrooms are necessarily an effeminate touch, can be refuted by the statement that so sturdy a soldier as the Great Napoleon had his dressing room at Fontainebleau lined with them! This fact reminds us that we have recently seen a most fascinating bathroom, planned for a woman, in which the walls and ceiling are of glass, cut in squares and fitted together in the old French way. Over the glass was a dull-gold trellis and twined in and out of this, ivy, absolutely natural in appearance, but made of painted tin. The floor tiles, and fixtures were white enamel, and a soft moss-green velvet carpet was laid down when the bath was not used.

Bathroom fixtures are to-day so elaborate in number and quality, that the conveniences one gets are limited only by one's purse. The leading manufacturers have anticipated the dreams of the most luxurious.

Window-curtains for bathrooms should be made of some material which will neither fade nor pull out of shape when washed. We would suggest scrim, Swiss, or China silk of a good quality.

When buying bath-mats, bath-robes, bath-slippers, bath-towels, wash-cloths and hand-towels, it is easy to keep in mind the colour-scheme of your rooms, and by following it out, the general appearance of your suite is immensely improved.

For a woman's bathroom, Venetian glass bottles, covered jars and bowls of every size, come in opalescent pale greens and other delicate tints. *See Plate XI*. Then there are the white glass bottles, jars, bowls, and trays with bunches of dashing pink roses, to be obtained at any good department store. Glass toilet articles come in considerable variety and at all prices, and to match any colour scheme; so use them as notes of colour on the glass shelves in your bathrooms. Here, too, is an opportunity to use your old Bristol or Bohemian glass, once regarded as inherited eyesores, but now unearthed, and which, when used to contribute to a colour scheme, have a distinct value and real beauty.

PLATE XVI

Part of a room in a small suite where the furniture is all old and the majority of it Empire in style. However, the small piano at once declares itself American Empire. The beautifully decorative nameplate on its front reads, "Geib & Walker, 23 Maiden Lane, N.Y." The date of piano is about 1830.

The brown mahogany commode on the right has the lion's claw-feet, and pilasters are topped by women's heads in bronze. This piece was bought in France. It has the original marble top, dark pink veined with white. The knobs on drawers are bronze lions' heads, holding rings in their mouths. Chairs are Italian and between Directoire and Empire.

The table, a good specimen, was also found in France. On the table is a French vanity mirror, Louis XVI in time, very Greek in design. The mirror is on both sides and turns on a gold arrow which pierces it. The bronze frame of mirror has a design so intricate in detail that it resembles lace work.

The vase on the piano is Empire and antique, decoration of green and gold. The flowers on table are artificial, a quaint Victorian contrast.

Through the doorway one sees the end of an Empire bed which came from an old château in Brittany. Note the same pilasters as on bureau, only that in this case the woman's head is gilded wood and two little feet of gilded wood appear at base of mahogany pilaster.

A gilded urn rests on a mahogany post of bed against the wall, the only position possible for beds of this style. The head and foot board are of equal height and alike.

Few Empire beds are now on the market. This one is used with a roll at each end and is covered with genuine Empire satin in six-inch stripes of canary yellow and sage green divided by two narrow black stripes and a narrow white stripe between them.

Corner of a Room in a Small Empire Suite

To-day a bathroom is considered the necessary supplement to every bedroom in an apartment or house, where the space allows, and no house is regarded as a good investment if built with less than one bath to communicate with every two rooms. Yet among the advertisements in the New York City Directory of 1828 we read the following naïve statement concerning warm baths, which is meant in all seriousness. It refers to the "Arcade Bath" at 32 Chambers Street, New York City.

***

"The warm bath is more conducive to health than any luxury which can be employed in a populous city; its beneficial effects are partially described as follows:

"The celebrated Count Rumford has paid particular attention to the subject of Warm Bathing; he has examined it by the test of experiments, long and frequently repeated, and bears testimony to its excellent effects. 'It is not merely on account of the advantages,' says the count, 'which I happen to see from Warm Bathing, which renders me so much an advocate of the practice; exclusive of the wholesomeness of the warm bath, the luxury of bathing is so great, and the tranquil state of the mind and body which follows, is so exquisitely delightful, that I think it quite impossible to recommend it too highly, if we consider it merely as a rational and elegant refinement. The manner in which the warm bath operates, in producing the salutary consequences, seems very evident. The genial warmth which is so applied to the skin in the place of the cold air of the atmosphere, by which we are commonly surrounded, expands all those very small vessels, where the extremities of the arteries and veins unite, and by gently stimulating the whole frame, produces a full and free circulation, which if continued for a certain time, removes all obstructions in the vascular system, and puts all the organs into that state of regular, free, and full motion which is essential to health, and also to that delightful repose, accompanied by a consciousness of the power of exertion, which constitutes the highest animal enjoyment of which we are capable.'

"N.B.: As the Bath is generally occupied on Saturday evenings and Sunday mornings, it is recommended to those who would wish to enjoy the Bath and avoid the crowded moment, to call at other times. The support of the public will be gratefully received and every exertion made to deserve it. For the Proprietor, G. Wright.

"Strangers will recognise the Bathing House from the front being extended over two lots of ground, and the centre basement being of free-stone."

***

The bathtub then was the simple tin sort, on the order of the round English tub. To-day the variety of bathtubs as to size, shape, material and appointments is bewildering; tubs there are on feet and tubs without feet, tubs sunken in the floor so that one goes down steps into them, tubs of large dimensions and tubs of small, and all with or without "showers," as the purchaser may prefer. Truly the warm baths so highly recommended in Count Rumford's rhapsody are to be had for the turning of one's own faucet at any moment of the day or night!

The Count Rumford in question is that romantic figure, born of simple English parents, in New England (Woburn, Mass., 1753), who went abroad when very young and by the great force of his personality and genius, became the power behind the throne in Bavaria, where he was made Minister of War and Field Marshal by the Elector, and later knighted in recognition of his scientific attainments and innumerable civic reforms. There is a large monument erected to the memory of Count Rumford in Munich. He died at Auteuil, France, in 1814.

CHAPTER XIII

PERIOD ROOMS

We use the term "period rooms" with full knowledge of the difficulties involved, in defining Louis XIV, Louis XV, Louis XVI, Directoire, Jacobean, Empire, Georgian, Victorian and Colonial decorations. Each period certainly has its distinctive earmarks in line and typical decoration, but you must realise that a period gradually evolves, at first exhibiting characteristics of its ancestors, then as it matures, showing a definite *new* type, and, later, when the elation of success has worn off, yielding to various foreign influences. By way of example, note the Chinese decoration on some of the painted furniture of the Louis XVI type, the Dutch influence on Chippendale in line, and the Egyptian on Empire.

One fascinating way of becoming familiar with history, is to delve into the origin and development of periods in furniture. The story of Napoleon is recorded in the unpretentious Directoire, the ornate Empire of Fontainebleau, while the conversion of round columns into obelisk-like pilasters surmounted by heads, the bronze and gilded-wood ornaments in the form of the Sphynx, are frank souvenirs of Egypt.

Every period, whether ascribed to England, France, Italy or Holland, has found expression in all adjacent countries. An Italian Louis XVI chair, mirror or applique is frequently sold in Paris or London as French and Empire furniture was "made in Germany." Periods have no restricted nationality; but nationality often declares itself in periods. That is to say, lines may be copied; but workmanship is another thing. Apropos of this take the French Empire furniture, massive as much of it is, built squarely and solidly to the floor, but showing most extraordinary grace on account of the amazing delicacy of intricate designs, done by the greatest French sculptors of the time and worked out in metal by the trained hands of men who had a special genius for this art. At no other time, nor in any other country, has an equal degree of perfection in the fine chiselling of metals so much as approached the standard attained during the Louis[1] and the Empire periods. If in your wandering, you happen upon a genuine bit of this work in silver or ormoulu, buy it.

---

[1] Louis XIV, XV, and XVI.

The writer once found in a New Jersey antique shop, a rare Empire bronze vase, urn-shaped, a specimen of the very finest kind of this metal engraving. The price asked for it (in ignorance, of course) was $2.50! The piece would have brought $40 in Paris. But the quest of the antique is another story.

When one realises the eternal borrowing of one country from another, the ever-recurring renaissance of past periods and the legitimate and illegitimate mixing of styles, it is no wonder that the amateur feels nervously uncertain, or frankly ignorant. Many a professional decorator hesitates to give a final judgment.

To take one case in point, we glibly speak of "Colonial" furniture, that term which covers such a multitude of sins, and inspiring virtues, too! We have the Colonial which closely resembles the Empire, and we have what is sometimes styled the Chippendale Colonial, following the Chippendale of England. Our Colonial cabinet-makers used as models, beautiful pieces imported from England, Holland and France by the wealthier members of our communities. Also a Chinese and Japanese influence crept in, on account of the lacquer and carved teak wood, brought home by our seafaring ancestors. It is quite possible that the carved teak wood stimulated the clever maker of some of the most beautiful Victorian furniture made in America, which is gradually finding its way into the hands of collectors. Some of these cabinet-makers glued together and put under heavy pressure seven to nine layers of rosewood with the grain running at every angle, so as to produce strength. When the layers had been crushed into a solid block, they carved their open designs, using one continuous piece of wood for the ornamental rim of even large sofas. The best of the Victorian period is attractive, but how can we express our opinion of those American monstrosities of the sixties or seventies, beds in rosewood and walnut, the head-boards covering the side of a room, bureaus proportionately huge, following out the idea that a piece of furniture to be beautiful must be very large and very expensive! It is to be hoped that the lovely rosewood and walnut wasted at that time are to-day being rescued by wary cabinet-makers.

The art of furniture making, like every other art, came into being to serve a clearly defined purpose. This must not be forgotten. A chair and a sofa are to sit on; a mirror, to *reflect*. Remember this last fact when hanging one. It is important that your mirror reflect one of the most attractive parts of your room, and thus contribute its quota to your scheme of decoration. It is interesting to note that chairs were made with solid wooden seats when men wore armour, velvet cushions followed more fragile raiment, and tapestries while always mural decorations were first used in place of doors and partitions, in feudal castles, before there were interior doors and partitions. Any piece of furniture is artistically bad when it does not satisfactorily serve its purpose. The equally fundamental law that everything useful should at the same time be beautiful cannot be repeated too often.

Period rooms which slavishly repeat, in every piece of furniture and ornament, only one type, have but a museum interest. If your rooms are to serve as a home, give them a winning, human quality, keep before your mind's eye, not royal palaces which have become museums, but *homes*, built and furnished by men and women whose traditions and associations gave them standards of beauty, so that they bought the choicest furniture both at home and abroad. In such a home, whether it be an intimate palace in Europe, a Colonial mansion in New England, or a Victorian interior of the best type, an extraneous period is often represented by some *objet d'art* as a delightful, because harmonious note of contrast.

For example, in a Louis XVI salon, where the colour scheme is harmonious, one gradually realises that one of the dominant ornaments in the room is a rare old Chinese vase, brought back from the Orient by one of the family and given a place of honour on account of its uniqueness.

Every one understands and feels deeply the difference between the museum palace or the period rooms of the commonplace decorator, and such a marvellous, living, breathing, palatial home as that "Italian palace" in Boston, Massachusetts, created, not inherited, by Mrs. John L. Gardner. Here we have a splendid example to illustrate the point we are trying to make; namely, regardless of its dimensions, make your home *home-like* and like *you*, its owner. Never allow any one, professional or amateur, to persuade you to put anything in it which you do not like yourself; but if an expert advises against a thing, give careful consideration to the advice before rejecting it. Mrs. Gardner's house is unique among the great houses of America as having that quality of the intimate palaces abroad,—a subtle mellowness which in the old world took time and generations of cultivated lovers of the rare and beautiful, to create. Adequate means, innate art appreciation, experience and the knowledge which comes from keeping in touch with experts, account for the intrinsic value of Mrs. Gardner's collection; but the subtle quality of harmony and vitality is her own personal touch. The colour scheme is so wisely chosen that it actually does unite all periods and countries. One is surprised to note how perfectly at home even the modern paintings appear in this version of an old Italian palace.

Be sure that you aim at the same combination of beauty, usefulness, and harmony between colour scheme and *objets d'art*. It is in colour scheme that we feel the personality of our host or hostess, therefore give attention to this point. Always have a colour scheme sympathetic to *you*. Make your rooms take on the air of being your abode. It is really very simple. What has been done with vast wealth can be just as easily done by the man of one room and a bath. Know what you want, and buy the best you can afford; by best, meaning useful things, indisputably beautiful in line and colour. Use your Colonial furniture; but if you find a wonderful Empire desk, with beautiful brass mounts and like it, buy it. They are of the same period in point of date, as it happens, and your Louis XVI bronze candlesticks will add a touch of grace. The writer recalls a simple room which was really a milestone in the development of taste, for it was so completely harmonious in colouring, arrangement of furniture, and placing of ornaments. Built for a painter's studio, with top light, it was used, at the time of which we speak, for music, as a Steinway grand indicated. The room was large, the floors painted black and covered with faded Oriental rugs; woodwork and walls were dark-green, as were the long, low, open bookcases, above which a large foliage tapestry was hung. On the other walls were modern paintings with antique frames of dulled gold, while a Louis XVI inlaid desk stood across one corner, and there was an old Italian oval table of black wood, with great, gold birds, as pedestal and legs, at which we dined simply, using fine old silver, and foreign pottery. This room was responsible for starting more than one person on the pursuit of the antique, for pervading it was a magic atmosphere, that wizard touch which comes of *knowing, loving* and *demanding beautiful things*, and then treating them very humanly. Use your lovely vases for your flowers. Hang your modern painting; but let its link with the faded tapestry be the dull, old frame. To be explicit, use lustreless frames and faded colours with old furniture and tapestry. Your grandmother wears mauves and greys—not bright red.

If your taste is for modern painted furniture and vivid Bakst colours in cushions and hangings, take your lovely old tapestry away. Speaking of tapestries, do not imagine that they can never be used in small rooms and narrow halls. <u>Plate XIV</u> shows an illustration of a hall in an old-fashioned country house, that was so narrow that it aroused despair. We call attention to the fact that it gains greatly in width from the perspective shown in the tapestry, one of the rare, old, painted kind, which depicts distance, wide vistas and a scene flooded with light. (An architectural picture can often be used with equally good results.) To increase size of this hall, the woodwork, walls and carpets were kept the same shade of pale-grey. The landscape paper in our Colonial houses of the eighteenth and early nineteenth centuries, often large in design, pushed back the walls to the same amazing degree.

CHAPTER XIV

PERIODS IN FURNITURE

Periods in furniture are amazingly interesting if one plunges into the story, not with tense nerves, but gaily, for mere amusement, and then floats gently, in a drifting mood. One gathers in this way many sparkling historical anecdotes, and much substantial data really not so cumbersome as some imagine!

To know anything at all about a subject one must begin at the beginning, and to make the long run seems a mere spin in an auto, let us at once remind you that the whole fascinating tale lies between the covers of one delightful book, the "Illustrated History of Furniture," by Frederick Litchfield, published by Truslove & Hanson, London, and by John Lane, New York. There are other books—many of them—but first exhaust Litchfield and apply what he tells you as you wander through public and private collections of furniture.

If you care for furniture at all, this book, which tells all that is known of its history, will prove highly instructive.

One cannot speak of the gradual development of furniture and furnishing; it is more a case of *waves of types*, and the story begins on the crest of a wave in Assyria, about 3000 years before Christ! Yes, seriously, interior decoration was an art back in that period and can be traced without any lost links in the chain of evidence.

From Assyria we turn to Egypt and learn from the frescoes and bas-reliefs on walls of ruined tombs, that about that same time, 3000 B.C., rooms on the banks of the Nile were decorated more or less as they are to-day. The cultured classes had beautiful ceilings, gilded furniture, cushions and mattresses of dyed linen and wools, stuffed with downy feathers taken from water fowl, curtains that were suspended between columns, and, what is still more interesting to the lover of furniture, we find that the style known as Empire when revived by Napoleon I was at that time in vogue. Even more remarkable is the fact that parts of legs and rails of furniture were turned as perfectly (I quote Litchfield) as if by a modern lathe. The variety of beautiful woods used by the Egyptians for furniture included ebony, cedar, sycamore and acacia. Marquetry was employed as well as wonderful inlaying with ivory, from both the elephant and hippopotamus. Footstools had little feet made like lion's claws or bull's hoofs. According to Austin Leyard, the very earliest Assyrian chairs, as well as those of Egypt, had the legs terminating in the same lion's feet or bull's hoofs, which reappear in the Greek, Roman, Empire and even Sheraton furniture of England (eighteenth century).

The first Assyrian chairs were made without backs and of beautifully wrought gold and bronze, an art highly developed at that time. In Egypt we find the heads of animals capping the backs of chairs in the way that we now see done on Spanish chairs.

The pilasters shown on the Empire furniture, *Plate XVI*, capped by women's heads with little gold feet at base, and caryatides of a kind, were souvenirs of the Egyptian throne seats which rested on the backs of slaves—possibly prisoners of war. These chairs were wonderful works of art in gold or bronze. We fancy we can see those interiors, the chairs and beds covered with woven materials in rich colours and leopard skins thrown over chairs, the carpets of a woven palm-fibre and mats of the same, which were used as seats.

Early Egyptian rooms were beautiful in line because simple; never crowded with superfluous furnishings. It is amusing to see on the very earliest bas-reliefs Egyptian belles and beaux reclining against what we know to-day as Empire rolls,—seen also on beds in old French prints of the fourteenth century. Who knows, even with the Egyptians this may have been a revived style!

One talks of new notes in colour scheme. The Bakst thing was being done in Assyria, 700 B.C.! Sir George Green proved it when he opened up six rooms of a king's palace and found the walls all done in horizontal stripes of red, yellow and green! Also, he states that each entrance had the same number of pilasters. Oh wise Assyrian King and truly neutral, if as is supposed, those rooms were for his six wives!

In furniture, the epoch-making styles have been those showing *line*, and if decorated, then only with such decorations as were subservient to line; pure Greek and purest Roman, Gothic and early Renaissance, the best of the Louis, Directoire and First Empire, Chippendale, Adam, Sheraton and Heppelwhite.

The bad styles are those where ornamentations envelop and conceal line as in late Renaissance, the Italian Rococo, the Portuguese Barrocco (baroque), the curving and contorted degenerate forms of Louis XIV and XV and the Victorian—all examples of the same thing, *i.e.*: perfect line achieved, acclaimed, flattered, losing its head and going to the bad in extravagant exuberance of over-ornamentation.

There is a psychic connection between the *outline* of furniture and the *inline* of man.

Perfect line, chaste ornamentation, the elimination of the superfluous was the result of the Greek idea of restraint—self-control in all things and in all expression. The immense authority of the law-makers enforced simple austerity as the right and only setting for the daily life of an Athenian, worthy of the name. There were exceptions, but as a rule all citizens, regardless of their wealth and station, had impressed upon them the civic obligation to express their taste for the beautiful, in the erecting of public buildings in their city of Athens, monuments of perfect art, by God-like artists, Phidias, Apelles, and Praxiteles.

CHAPTER XV

CONTINUATION OF PERIODS IN FURNITURE

From Greece, culture, borne on the wings of the arts, moved on to Rome, and at first, Roman architecture and decoration reproduced only the classic Greek types; but, as Rome grew, her arts took on another and very different outline, showing how the history of decorative art is to a fascinating degree the history of customs and manners.

Rome became prosperous, greedy, powerful and imperious, enslaving the civilised world, and, not having the restraining laws of Greece, waxed luxurious and licentious, and chafed, in consequence, at the austere rigidity of the Greek style of furnishing.

We know that in the time of Augustus Cæsar the Romans had wonderful furniture of the most costly kind, made from cedar, pine, elm, olive, ash, ilex, beach and maple, carved to represent the legs, feet, hoofs and heads of animals, as in earlier days was the fashion in Assyria, Egypt and Greece, while intricate carvings in relief, showed Greek subjects taken from mythology and legend. Cæsar, it is related, owned a table costing a million sesterces ($40,000).

But gradually the pure line swerved, ever more and more influenced by the Orient, for Rome, always successful in war, had established colonies in the East. Soon Byzantine art reached Rome, bringing its arabesques and geometrical designs, its warm, glowing colours, soft cushions, gorgeous hangings, embroideries, and rich carpets. In fact all the glowing luxury that the *new* Roman craved.

The effect of this *mésalliance* upon all Art, including interior decoration, was to cause its immediate decline. Elaboration and *banal* designs, too much splendour of gold and silver and ivory inlaid with gold, resulted in a decadent art which reflected a decadent race and Rome fell! Not all at once; it took five hundred years for the neighbouring races to crush her power, but continuous hectoring did it, in 476 A.D. Then began the Dark Ages merging into the Middle Ages (fifth to fifteenth centuries).

Dark they were, but what picturesque and productive darkness! Rome fell, but the Carlovingian family arose, and with it the great nations of Western Europe, to give us, especially in France, another supreme flowering of interior decoration. Britain was torn from the grasp of Rome by the Saxons, Danes and Normans, and as a result the great Anglo-Saxon race was born to create art periods. Mahomet appeared and scored as an epoch-maker, recording a remarkable life and a spiritual cycle. The Moors conquered Spain, but in so doing enriched her arts a thousandfold, leaving the Alhambra as a beacon-light through the ages. Finally the crusades united all warring races against the infidels. Blood was shed, but at the same time routes were opened up, by which the arts, as well as the commerce, of the Orient, reached Europe. And so the Byzantine continued to contend with Gothic art—that art which preceded from the Christian Church and stretched like a canopy over Western Europe, all through the Middle Ages. It was in the churches and monasteries that Christian art, driven from pillar to post by wars, was obliged to take refuge, and there produced that marvellous development known as the Gothic style,—of the Church, for the Church, by the Church, perfected in countless Gothic cathedrals,—crystallised glorias lifting their manifold spires to heaven,—ethereal monuments of an intrepid Faith which gave material form to its adoration, its fasting and prayer, in an unrivalled art.

There is one early Gothic chair which has come down to us, Charlemagne's, made of gilt-bronze and preserved in the Louvre, at Paris. Any knowledge beyond this one piece, as to what Carlovingian furniture was like (the eighth century) we get only from old manuscripts which show it to have been the pseudo-classic, that is, the classic modified by Byzantine influence, and very like the Empire style of Napoleon I. Here is the reason for the type. Constantinople was the capital of the Eastern Empire, when in 726 A.D., Emperor Leo III prohibited image worship, and the artists and artisans of his part of the world, in order to earn a livelihood, scattered over Europe, settling in the various capitals, where they were eagerly welcomed and employed.

Even so late as the tenth to fourteenth centuries the knowledge we have of Gothic furniture still comes from illustrated manuscripts and missals preserved in museums or in the national libraries.

Rome fell as an empire in the fifth century. In the eighth century, Venice asserted herself, later becoming the great, wealthy, Merchant City of Eastern Europe, the golden gate between Byzantium and the West (eleventh to fifteenth centuries). Her merchants visiting every country naturally carried home all art expressions, but, so far as we know, her own chief artistic output in very early days, was in the nature of richly carved wooden furniture, no specimens of which remain.

CHAPTER XVI

THE GOTHIC PERIOD

The Gothic Period is the pointed period, and dominated the art of Europe from about the tenth to the fifteenth century. Its origin was Teutonic, its development and perfection French.

At first, the house of a feudal lord meant one large hall with a raised dais, curtained off for him and his immediate family, and subdivided into sleeping apartments for the women. On this dais a table ran crossways, at which the lord and his family with their guests, ate, while a few steps lower, at a long table running lengthwise of the hall, sat the retainers. The hall was, also, the living-room for all within the walls of the castle. Sand was strewn on the stone floor and the dogs of the knights ate what was thrown to them, gnawing the bones at their leisure. This rude scene was surrounded by wonderful tapestries hung from the walls:—woman's record of man's deeds.

Later, we read of stairs and of another room known as the *Parloir* or talking-room, and here begins the sub-division of homes, which in democratic America has arrived at a point where more than 200 rooms are often sheltered under one private roof!

Oak chests figured prominently among the furnishings of a Gothic home, because the possessions of those feudal lords, who were constantly at war with one another, often had to be moved in haste. As men's lives became more settled, their possessions gradually multiplied; but even at the end of the eleventh century bedsteads were provided only for the nobility, probably on account of expense, as they were very grand affairs, carved and draped. To that time and later belong the wonderfully carved presses or wardrobes.

Carved wood panelling was an important addition to interior decoration during the reign of Henry III (1216-72).

In the thirteenth and fourteenth centuries England with Flanders led in the production of mediæval art.

Hallmarks of the Gothic period are animals and reptiles carved to ornament the structural parts of furniture and to ornament panels. Favourite subjects with the wood carvers of that time were scenes from the lives of the saints (the Church dominated the State) and from the romances, chanted by the minstrels.

CHAPTER XVII

THE RENAISSANCE

Following the Gothic Period came the Renaissance of Greek art which began in Italy under the leadership of Leonardo Da Vinci and Raphael, who, rejecting the existing types of degraded decorative art, in Italy a combination of the Byzantine and Gothic—turned to the antique, the purest Greek styles of Pericles' time. The result was another period of perfect line and proportion, called the Italian Renaissance, a great wave of art which swept over all Europe, gaining impetus from the wise patronage of the ruling Medicis. One of them (Pope Leo X with the co-operation of Italy's reigning dukes and princes) employed and so developed the extraordinary powers of Michael Angelo, Titian, Raphael, Andrea del Sarto and Correggio.

By the end of the fifteenth century, Classic Greek art was engrossing the mind of Western Europe, classical literature was becoming the fashion and there was even an attempt to make Latin the popular language.

It was during the Renaissance that Palladio rebuilt the palaces of Italy,—beautiful beyond words, and that Benvenuto Cellini designed in gold, silver and bronze in a manner never since equalled. From that same period dates the world-famous Majolica of Urbino, Pesaro and Gubbio, shown in our museums. So far as house-furnishing went, aside from palaces, there was but little that was appropriate for intimate domestic life. The early Renaissance furniture was palatial, architectural in outline and, one might almost say, in proportions. The tables were impossibly high, the chairs were stiff, and the cabinets immense and formal in outline. It had, however, much stately beauty, and very lovely are certain old pieces of carved and gilded wood where the gilt, put on over a red preparation and highly burnished, has rubbed off with time, and shows a soft glow of colour through the gold.

But as always, the curse of over-elaboration to please perverted minds, was resorted to by cabinet-makers who copied mosaics with their inlaying, and invented that form known as *pietra-dura*—polished bits of marble, agates, pebbles and lapis lazuli. Ivory was carved and used as bas-reliefs and ivory and tortoise shell, brass and mother-of-pearl used as inlay. Elaborate

Arabesque designs inlaid were souvenirs of the Orient, and where the cabinetmaker's saw left a line, the cuts were filled in with black wood or stained glue, which brought out the design and so gave an added decorative effect. Skilled artisans had other designs bitten into wood by acids, and shading was managed by pouring hot sand on the surface of the wood. Hallmarks of the Renaissance are designs which were taken from Greek and Roman mythology, and allegories representing the elements, seasons, months and virtues. Also, battle scenes and triumphal marches.

    The insatiable love for decoration found still another expression in silver and gold plaques of the highest artistic quality, embossed and engraved for those princes of Florence, Urbino, Ferrara, Rome, Venice and Naples, who vied with one another in extravagance until the inevitable reaction came.

PLATE XVII

An example of good mantel decoration. The vases and clock are Empire, the chairs Directoire, and footstools Louis XV.

A low bowl of modern green Venetian glass holds flowers.

An Example of Perfect Balance and Beauty in Mantel Arrangement

Edmund Bonneffé says that in the latter part of the Renaissance, while the effort of the Italians seems to have been to disguise wood, French cabinet-makers emphasised its value—an interesting point to bear in mind.

If we trace the Renaissance movement in Germany we find that it was Albrecht Dürer who led it. Then, as always, the Germans were foremost in wood carving; with Holland and Belgium they are responsible for much of the antique oak furniture on Renaissance lines. The Scandinavians have also done wonderful wood carving, which is easily confused with the early wood carving of the Russians, for the reason that the Swedes settled Finland, and Russia's Ruric rulers (before the Romanoff house,—sixteenth century) were from Finland.

In the sixteenth century metal work in steel, iron and brass reached its height in Germany and Italy. It is supposed that the elaborate mounts in furniture which were later perfected in France had their origin in iron corners and hinge-plates used, at first, merely to strengthen, but as the men who worked in metals became more and more skilful, the mounts were made with the intent of mere decoration and to draw attention to the beauty of the wood itself.

Before Dürer turned Germany's mind toward the Greek revival of Art, the craftsmen of his country had been following Dutch models. This was natural enough, for Charles V was king at that time, of Holland, Germany and Spain, and the arts of the three countries, as well as their commerce were interchangeable. In fact it was the Dutch painter, Van Eyck, who took the Renaissance into Spain when called thereto paint royalty. Sculptors, tapestry weavers, books on art, etc., followed.

That was the Spanish awakening, but the art of Spain during the sixteenth century shows that the two most powerful influences were Moorish and Italian. The most characteristically Spanish furniture of that period are those cabinets,—"*Vargueos*," made of wood ornamented on the outside with wrought iron, while inside are little columns made of fine bone, painted and gilded. Much of the old Spanish furniture reproduces German and Italian styles. Embossed leather put on with heavy nails has always been characteristic of Spain, and in the seventeenth century very fine Spanish mahogany and chestnut were decorated with tortoise-shell inlaid with ivory, so as to make elaborate pictures in the Italian style. (See Baron Davillier on Spanish Furniture.).

CHAPTER XVIII

FRENCH FURNITURE

The classic periods in French furniture were those known as Francis I, Henry II and the three Louis,—XIV, XV, and XVI. One can get an idea of all French periods in furnishing by visiting the collection in Paris belonging to the government, "Mobilier National," in the new wing of the Louvre.

It is always necessary to consult political history in order to understand artistic invasions. Turn to it now and you will find that Charles VIII of France held Naples for two years (1495-6), and when he went home took with him Italian artists to decorate his palaces. Read on and find that later Henry II married Catherine de Medici and loved Diane de Poitiers, and that, fortunately for France, both his queen and his mistress were patronesses of the arts. So France bloomed in the sunshine of royal favour and Greek influence, as few countries ever had. Fontainebleau (begun by Francis I) was the first of a chain of French royal palaces, all monuments without and within, to a picturesque system of monarchy,—Kings who could do no wrong, wafting sceptres over powerless subjects, whose toil produced Art in the form of architecture, cabinetmaking, tapestry weaving, mural decoration, unrivalled porcelain, exquisitely wrought silver and gold plate, silks, lovely as flower gardens (showing the "pomegranate" and "vase" patterns) and velvets like the skies! And for what? Did these things represent the wise planning of wise monarchs for dependent subjects? We know better, for it is only in modern times that simple living and small incomes have achieved surroundings of artistic beauty and comfort.

The marvels of interior decoration during the classic French periods were created for kings and their queens, mistresses and favoured courtiers. Diane de Poitiers wished—perhaps only dreamed—and an epoch-making art project was born. Madame du Barry admired and made her own the since famous du Barry rose colour, and the Sèvres porcelain factories reproduced it for her. But how to produce this particular illusive shade of deep, purplish-pink became a forgotten art, when the seductive person of the king's mistress was no more.

If you would learn all there is to know concerning the sixteenth century furnishings in France read Edmund Bonneffé's "Sixteenth Century Furniture."

It was the Henry II interior decoration and architecture which first showed the Renaissance of pure line and classic proportion, followed by the never-failing reaction from the simple line to the undulating over-ornate when decoration repeated the elaboration of the most luxurious, licentious periods of the past.

One has but to walk through the royal palaces of France to see French history beguilingly illustrated, in a series of volumes open to all, the pages of which are vibrant with the names and personalities of men and women who will always live in history as products of an age of great culture and art.

PLATE XVIII

A delightful bit of a room. The furniture, in line, shows a Directoire influence. The striped French satin sofa and one chair is blue, yellow and faun, the Brussels tapestry in faded blues, fauns and greys. Over a charmingly painted table is a Louis XV gilt applique, the screen is dark in tone and has painted panels.

The rug, done in cross-stitch, black ground and design colours, was discovered in a forgotten corner of a shop, its condition so dingy from the dust of ages that only an expert would have recognised its possibilities.

Corner of a Drawing Room, Furniture Showing Directoire influence

The Louis XIV, XV and XVI periods in furniture are all related. Rare brocades, flowered and in stripes, bronze mounts as garlands, bow-knots and rosettes, on intricate inlaying, mark their common relationship. The story of these periods is that gradually decoration becomes over-elaborated and in the end dominates the Greek outline.

The three Louis mark a succession of great periods. Louis XIV, though beautiful at its best, is of the three the most ornate and is characterised in its worst stage by the extremely bowed (cabriole) legs of the furniture, ludicrously suggestive of certain debauched courtiers who surrounded the *Grande Monarch*.

Louis XV legs show a curve, also, but no longer the stoggy, squat cabriole of the over-fed gallant. Instead we are entranced by an ethereal grace and lightness of movement in every line and decoration. Here cabriole means but a courtly knee swiftly bending to salute some beauty's hand. So subtly waving is the curving outline of this furniture that one scarcely knows where it begins or ends, and it is the same with the decorations—exquisitely delicate waving traceries of vines and flora, gold on gold, inlay, or paint in delicate tones. All this gives to the Louis XV period supremacy over Louis XVI, whose round, grooved, tapering straight legs, one tires of more quickly, although fine gold and lovely paint make this type winning and beloved.

From Louis XVI we pass to the Directoire, when, following the Revolution, the voice of the populace decried all ostentation and everything savouring of the superfluous. The Great Napoleon in his first period affected simplicity and there were no longer bronze mounts, in rosettes, garlands and bow-knots, elaborate inlaying, nor painted furniture with lovely flowering surfaces; in the most severe examples not even fluted legs! Instead, simple but delicately proportioned furniture with slender, squarely cut, chastely tapering legs, arms and backs, was the fashion. In fact, the Directoire type is one of ideal proportions, graceful outlines with a flowing movement and the decoration when present, kept well within bounds, entirely subservient to the main structural material. One feels an almost Quaker-like quality about the Directoire, whether of natural wood or plain painted surface.

With Napoleon's assumption of regal power and habits, we get the Empire (he had been to Rome and Egypt), pseudo-classic in outline and richly ornamented with mounts in ormoulu characteristic of the Louis.

The Empire period in furniture was dethroned by the succeeding régime.

When we see old French chairs with leather seats and backs, sometimes embossed, in the Portuguese style, with small regular design, put on with heavy nails and twisted or straight stretchers (pieces of wood extending between legs of chairs), we know that they belong to the time of Henry IV or Louis XIII. Some of the large chairs show the shell design in their broad, elaborate stretchers.

The beautiful small side tables of the Louis and First Empire called consoles, were made for the display of their marvellously wrought pieces of silver, hammered and chiselled by hand,—"museum pieces," indeed, and lucky is the collector who chances upon any specimen adrift.

CHAPTER XIX

THE PERIODS OF THE THREE LOUIS

The only way to learn how to distinguish the three *Louis* is to study these periods in collections of furniture and objects of art, or, where this is impossible, to go through books showing interiors of those periods. In this way one learns to visualise the salient features of any period and gradually to acquire a *feeling* for them, that subtle sense which is not dependent wholly upon outline, decoration, nor colour, but upon the combined result.

French writers who specialise along the lines of interior decoration often refer to the three types as follows:

Period of Louis XIV—heavily, stolidly masculine;
Period of Louis XV—coquettishly feminine;
Period of Louis XVI—lightly, alertly masculine.

One soon sees why, for Louis XIV furniture does suggest masculinity by its weight and size. It is squarely made, straight (classic) in line, equally balanced, heavily ponderous and magnificent. Over its surface, masses of decoration immobile as stone carving, are evenly dispersed, and contribute a grandiose air to all this furniture.

There was impressive gallantry to the Louis XIV style, a ceremonious masculine gallantry, while Louis XV furniture—the period dominated by women when "poetry and sculpture sang of love" and life revolved about the boudoir—shows a type entirely *intime*, sinuously, lightly, gracefully, coquettishly feminine, bending and courtesying, with no fixed outline, no equal balance of proportions. Louis XV was the period when outline and decoration were merged in one and the *shell* which figured in Louis XIV merely as an ornament, gave its form (in a curved outline) and its name "rococo" (Italian for shell) to the style.

As a reaction from this we get the Louis XVI period, again masculine in its straight rigidity of line, its perfectly poised proportions, the directness of its appeal to the eye, a "reflection of the more serious mental attitude of the nation." Louis XVI had an aristocratic sobriety and was masculine in a light, alert, mental way, if one can so express it, which stimulates the imagination, in direct contrast to the material and literal type of Louis XIV which, as we have said, was masculine in its ponderous magnificence, and unyielding over-ornamentation.

So much for *outline*. Now for the *decoration* of the three periods.

Remember that the Louis XIV, XV and XVI periods took their ideas for decoration from the Greeks, via Italy, and the extreme Orient. A national touch was added by means of their Sèvres porcelain medallions set into furniture, and the finely chiselled bronzes known as ormoulu, a superior alloy of metals of a rich gold colour. The subjects for these chiselled bronzes were taken from Greek and Roman mythology; gods, goddesses, and cupids the insignia of which were torches, quivers, arrows, and tridents. There were, also, wreaths, garlands, festoons and draperies, as well as rosettes, ribbons, bow-knots, medallion heads, and the shell and acanthus leaf. One finds these in various combinations or as individual motives on the furniture of the Louis.

PLATE XIX

Shows the red-tiled entrance hall of a duplex apartment in New York.

On the walls are two Italian mirrors (Louis XVI), a side table (console) of the same epoch, and two Italian carved chairs.

Entrance Hall in New York Duplex Apartment. Italian Furniture

The backgrounds for these mounts were the woods finely inlaid with ivory shell and brass in the style of the Italian Renaissance. Oriental lacquer and painted furniture, at that time heavily gilded.

The legs of chairs, sofas and tables of the Louis XIV period were cabrioles (curved outward)—a development of the animal legs of carved wood, bronze or gold, used by the ancient Assyrians, Egyptians and Greeks as supports for tables and chairs. Square grooved legs also appeared in this type.

The same grooves are found on round tapering legs of Louis XVI's time. In fact that type of leg is far more typical of the Louis XVI period than the cabriole or square legs grooved, but one sees all three styles.

Other hallmarks of the Louis XVI period are the straight outlines, perfectly balanced proportions, the rosettes, ribbon and bow-knot with torch and arrows in chiselled bronze.

That all "painting and sculpture sang of love" is as true of Louis XVI as of Louis XV. In both reigns the colouring was that of spring-tender greens, pale blossoms, the grey of mists, sky-blues, and yellows of sunshine.

During Louis XV's time soft cushions fitted into the sinuous lines of the furniture, and as some Frenchman has put it, "a vague, discreet perfume pervaded the whole period, in contrast to the heavier odour of the First Empire."

The walls and ceilings of the three Louis were richly decorated in accordance with a scheme, surpassing in magnificence any other period.

An intricate system of mouldings (to master which, students at the École des Beaux Arts, Paris, must devote years) encrusted sidewalls and ceilings, forming panels and medallions, over-doors and chimney-pieces, into which were let paintings by the great masters of the time, whose subjects reflected the moods and interests of each period. The Louis XV and XVI paintings are tender and vague as to subject and the colours veiled in a greyish tone, full of sentiment.

That was the great period of tapestry weaving—Beauvais, Arras and Gobelin, and these filled panels or hung before doors.

It may be said that the period of Louis XVI profited by antiquity, but continued French traditions; it was a renaissance of line and decoration kept alive, while the First Empire was classic form inanimate, because an abrupt innovation rather than an influence and a development. One may go farther and quote the French claim that the colour scheme of Louis XVI was intensely suggestive and personal, while the Empire colouring was literal and impersonal.

Under Louis XVI furniture was all but lost in a crowd of other articles, tapestry, draperies of velvet, flowered silks, little objects of art in porcelain, more or less useless, silver and ormoulu, exquisitely decorated with a précieuse intricacy of chiselled designs.

The Louis XVI period was rigid in its aristocratic sobriety, for although torch and arrows figured, as did love-birds, in decoration—(souvenirs of the painter Boucher), everything was set and decorous, even the arrow was often the warrior's not cupid's; in the same way the torch was that of the ancients, and when a medallion showed a pastoral subject, its frame of straight lines linked it to the period. Even if Cupid appeared, he was decorously framed or pedestaled.

To be sure, Marie Antoinette and the ladies of her court played at farming in the Park of the Petite Trainon, at Versailles; but they wore silk gowns and powdered wigs. To be rustic was the fad of the day (there was a cult for gardening in England); but shepherdesses were confined to tapestries, and, while the aristocracy held the stage, it played the game of life in gloves.

There was about the interior decoration of Louis XVI, as about the lives of aristocratic society of that time, a "penetrating perfume of love and gallantry," to which all admirers of the beautiful must ever return for refreshment and standards of beauty and grace.

Speaking generally of the three Louis one can say that on a background of a great variety of wonderful inlaid woods, ivory, shell, mother-of-pearl and brass, or woods painted and gilded, following the Italian Renaissance, or lacquered in the manner of the Orient, were ormoulu wrought and finely chiselled, showing Greek mythological subjects; gods, goddesses and their insignia, with garlands, wreaths, festoons, draperies, ribbons, bow-knots, rosettes and medallions of cameo, Sèvres porcelain, or Wedgwood paste. Among the lost arts of that time are inlaying as done by Boule and the finish known as Vernis Martin.

PLATE XX

This large studio is a marked example of comfort and interest where the laws of appropriateness, practicableness, proportion and balance are so observed as to communicate at once a sense of restfulness.

Here the comfortable antiques and beautifully proportioned modern furniture make an ideal combination of living-room and painter's studio.

Combination of Studio and Living Room in a New York Duplex Apartment

Tapestries and mural paintings were framed by a marvellous system of mouldings which covered ceilings and sidewalls.

The colour scheme was such as would naturally be dictated by the general mood of artificiality in an age when dreams were lived and the ruling classes obsessed by a passion for amusements, invented to divert the mind from actualities. This colour scheme was beautifully light in tone and harmoniously gay, whether in tapestries, draperies and upholstery of velvets, or flowered silks, frescoes or painted furniture. It had the appearance of being intended to act as a soporific upon society, whose aim it was to ignore those jarring contrasts which lay beneath the surface of every age.

CHAPTER XX

CHARTS SHOWING HISTORICAL EVOLUTION OF FURNITURE

LOUIS XIV,
  1643 to 1715
Key-note
  The Grand
    Audience Rooms

Compressed regularity giving way in reaction to a ponderous ugliness.

Straight, square, grooved and very squat cabriole legs.

THE REGENCY AND
LOUIS XV,
  1715 to 1774
Key-note
  The Boudoir

The Reign of Woman.

Cabriole legs of a perfect lightness and grace.

LOUIS XVI,
  1774 to 1793
Key-note
  The Salon *Intime*

The transition style between the Bourbon Interior Decoration and that of the "Directorate" and "Empire," characterised by a return to the classic line which reflects a more serious turn of mind on part of the Nation in an age of great mental activity.

Legs tapering straight, rounded and grooved. A few square-grooved legs and a few graceful, slender cabriole legs.

THE FIRST EMPIRE,

Classic lines.

NAPOLEON I, 1804 to 1814

Classic decorations with subjects taken from Greek mythologies.

Winged figures, emblems of liberty; antique heads of helmeted warriors, made like medallions, wreaths, lyres, torches, rosettes, etc.

Besides the wonderful mounts of Ormoulu, designed by the great sculptors and painters of the period, there was a great deal of fine brass inlaying.

Antique vases taken from ancient tombs were placed in recesses in the walls of rooms after the style of the ancient "Columbaria."

Every effort was made to surround Napoleon I with the dignity and austere sumptuousness of a great Roman Emperor. As we have said, he had been in Rome and he had been in Egypt; the art of the French Empire was reminiscent of both. Napoleon would outstrip the other conquerors of the world.

Some Empire furniture shows the same fine turning which characterizes Jacobean furniture of both oak and walnut periods. We refer to the round, not spiral, turning. See legs of Empire sofa on which Madame Récamier reclines in the well-known portrait by David (Louvre).

ENGLISH FURNITURE

THE OAK PERIOD   Gothic, through 14th Century.

ENGLISH FURNITURE

(including early Jacobean)	Renaissance, 16th Century Elizabethan, 16th Century. Jacobean or Stuart, 17th Century; James I, Charles I and II, and James II, 1603-1688.	
THE WALNUT PERIOD	Late Jacobean. William and Mary, 1688. Queen Anne, 1702.	
"MAHOGANY" PERIOD (and other imported woods), or, CHIPPENDALE PERIOD.	Chippendale. HEPPELWHITE. SHERATON THE ADAM BROTHERS.	18th Century.

GOTHIC PERIOD, Through 14th Century.	Almost no furniture exists of the 13th Century. We get the majority of our ideas from illustrated manuscripts of that time. The furniture was carved oak or plain oak ornamented with iron scroll work, intended both for strength and decoration.
RENAISSANCE OR ELIZABETHAN, 16th Century.	The characteristic, heavy, wide mouldings and small panels, and heavy round carving.
JACOBEAN OR STUART PERIOD, 17th Century. WALNUT PERIOD,	Panels large and mouldings very narrow and flat, or no mouldings at all, and flat carving. The classic influence shown during the period of the Commonwealth in designs, pilastars

ENGLISH FURNITURE

late 17th Century. and pediments was the result of a classic reaction, all elaboration being resented. The Restoration brought in elaborate carving. Dutch influence is exemplified in the fashion for inlaying imported from Holland, as well as the tulip design. Turned legs, stretchers, borders and spiral turnings, characterized Jacobean style.

In the GOTHIC PERIOD (extending through 14th Century), as the delightful irregularity in line and decoration shows, there was NO SET TYPE; each piece was an individual creation and showed the personality of maker.

Tables, chests, presses (wardrobes), chairs and benches or settles.

During RENAISSANCE OR ELIZABETHAN PERIOD (16th Century) types begin to establish and repeat themselves.

Table chests, presses, chairs, benches, settles, and small chests of drawers.

In the JACOBEAN (17th Century) there was already a set type, pieces made all alike, turned out by the hundreds.

Inlaying in ebony, ivory, mother-of-pearl, and ebonised oblong bosses of the jewel type (last half of 17th Century). The tulip design introduced from Holland as decoration.

Turned and carved frames and stretchers; caned seats and backs to chairs, velvet cushions, velvet satin damask and needlework upholstery, the seats stuffed.

Henry VIII made England *Protestant*, it having been Roman Catholic for several hundred years before the coming of the Anglo-Saxons and for a thousand years after.

PROTESTANT.   QUEEN ELIZABETH.
"The Elizabethan Period."

STUART.
ROMAN
CATHOLIC.   JAMES I. 1603.
"JACOBEAN." CHARLES I. (Puritan Revolution), 1628.

PURITAN.   Oliver Cromwell. 1649.
Commonwealth.

STUART.
ROMAN
CATHOLIC.   {Charles II. (1660), Restoration.
"JACOBEAN." James II. (1686), Deposition and Flight.

             William—Prince of Orange (Holland), 1688.
PROTESTANT. Who had married the English Princess Mary and was the only available *Protestant* (1688).

PROTESTANT. Queen Anne (1702-1714).

CHAPTER XXI

THE MAHOGANY PERIOD

It is interesting to note that the Great Fire of London started the importation of foreign woods from across the Baltic, as great quantities were needed at once for the purpose of rebuilding. These soft woods aroused the invention of the cabinet-makers, and were especially useful for inlaying; so we find in addition to oak, that mahogany, pear and lime woods were used in fine furniture, it being lime-wood that Grinling Gibbons carved when working with Sir Christopher Wren, the famous architect (seventeenth century).

During the early Georgian period the oak carvings were merely poor imitations of Elizabethan and Stuart designs. There seemed to have been no artist wood-carvers with originality, which may have been partly due to a lack of stimulus, as the fashion in the decoration of furniture turned toward inlaying.

THE PERIOD OF WILLIAM III AND QUEEN MARY AND EARLY GEORGIAN

are characterised by turned work, giving way to flattened forms, and the disappearance of the elaborate front stretcher on Charles II chairs.

The coming of mahogany into England and its great popularity there gives its name to that period when Chippendale, Heppelwhite, Sheraton and the Adam Brothers were the great creative cabinet-makers. The entire period is often called CHIPPENDALE, because Chippendale's books on furniture, written to stimulate trade by arousing good taste and educating his public, are considered the best of that time. There were three editions: 1754, 1759, and 1762.

The work was entitled "The Gentleman and Cabinet-maker's Director and Useful Designs of Household Furniture in the Gothic, Chinese and Modern Taste" (and there was still more to the title!).

Chippendale's genius lay in taking the best wherever he found it and blending the whole into a type so graceful, beautiful, perfectly proportioned, light in weight and appearance, and so singularly suited to the uses for which it was intended, that it amounted to creation.

The "Chinese Craze" in England was partly due to a book so

called, written by Sir William Chambers, architect, who went to China and not only studied, but sketched, the furniture, he saw there.

Thomas Sheraton, we are assured, was the most cultivated of this group of cabinet-makers. The three men made both good and bad styles. The work of the three men can be distinguished one from the other and, also, it can be very easily confused. To read up a period helps; but to really know any type of furniture with certainty, one must become familiar with its various and varying characteristics.

The houses and furniture designed and made by the Adam brothers were an epoch in themselves. These creations were the result of the co-operation of a little band of artists, consisting of Michael Angelo Pergolesi, who published in 1777, "Designs for Various Ornaments"; Angelica Kauffman and Cipriani, two artist-painters who decorated the walls, ceilings, woodwork and furniture designed by the Adam brothers; and another colleague, the great Josiah Wedgwood, whose medallions and plaques, cameo-like creations in his jasper paste, showed both classic form and spirit.

The Adam brothers' creations were rare exotics, with no forerunners and no imitators, like nothing the world had ever seen—yet reflecting the purest Greek period in line and design.

One of the characteristics of the Mahogany Period was the cabriole leg, which is, also, associated with Italian and French furniture of the seventeenth and eighteenth centuries. As a matter of fact this form of leg is as old as the Romans and is really the same as the animal legs of wood or bronze, used as supports for tripods and tables by Assyrians, Egyptians and Greeks. The cabriole leg may be defined as "a convex curve above a concave one, with the point of junction smoothed away. On Italian console tables and French commodes we see the two simple curves disguised by terminal figures."

The rocaille (shell) ornament on the Chippendale as well as the cabriole leg copied from Italy and France, and the Dutch foot from Holland, substantiate our claim that Chippendale used what he found wherever he found it irrespective of the stigma of plagiarism.

There is a beautiful book by F.S. Robinson in which the entire subject of English furniture is treated in a most charming fashion.

Now let us return a moment to the Jacobean period. It was under Charles I that couches and settles became prominent pieces of furniture. Some of the Jacobean chairs are like those made in Italy, in the seventeenth century, with crossed legs, backs and seats covered with red velvet. Other Jacobean chairs had scrollwork carved and pierced, with central panel in the back of embroidery, while the seat was of cane.

Some of the Jacobean cabinets had panels of ebony, the other parts inlaid with mother-of-pearl and ivory.

The silver Jacobean furniture is interesting and the best examples of this type are said to be those belonging to Lord Sackville. They are of ebony with silver mountings.

Yorkshire is noted for its Jacobean furniture, but some famous rooms done in this style are at Langleys, in Essex, the seat of Col. Tufnell, where the ceilings and mantels are especially fine and the library boasts interesting panelled walls, once enlivened by stained glass windows, when this room was used as a private chapel for the family.

Jacobean carving was never ornate.

Twenty years later came the Queen Anne period. Queen Anne chairs show a solid splat, sometimes vase-shaped, and strap-work arabesques. Most of the legs were cabriole, instead of the twisted turnings (on Stuart lines) which had been Supports for chairs, cabinets and tables. The Queen Anne chair legs terminated when cabriole, in claws and balls or simple balls. Settees for two were then called "love seats," and "pole-screens" belonged to this period, tall, slender poles with small, sliding screens.

Queen Anne hangings were of rich damasks, silks and velvets, and the wainscot of rooms was painted some pale colour as an effective background to set off the dark, turned walnut or gorgeous lacquer made in red, green or black, and ornamented with gold. Some of the Queen Anne pieces of this variety had hinges and lockplates of chased brass. Another variety was of oak, veneered with walnut and inlaid.

The very high ceilings of the Queen Anne period led to the use of "tall boys" or family bureaus, those many-storied conveniences which comprised a book-case above, writing desk in the middle, and drawers below.

Lockwood says in giving the history of chairs, in his "Cabinet Makers from 1750 to 1840": "Extravagance of taste and fluctuation of fashion had reached high water mark due to increase of wealth in England and her colonies. From the plain, stately pieces of Queen Anne the public turned to the rococo French designs of early Chippendale, then tiring of that, veered back to classic lines, as done by the Adam brothers, and so on, from heavy Chippendale to the overlight and perishable Heppelwhite. Then public taste turned to the gaudily painted Sheraton and finally, took to copying the French Empire."

The American Revolutionary War stopped the exportation of furniture to America, with the result that cabinet-makers in the United States copied Chippendale and neglected all other later artists. When America began again to import models, Sheraton was an established and not a transitional type. Beautiful specimens are shown in the Nichols house, at Salem, Mass., furnished in 1783. The furniture used by George Washington when President of the United States in 1789, and now in the City Hall, New York, is pure Sheraton. (See Colonial Furniture, Luke Vincent Lockwood.)

Sir Christopher Wren, architect, with Grinling Gibbons, designer and wood-carver, were chiefly responsible for the beautifully elaborate mouldings on ceilings and walls, carved from oak and used for forming large panels with wide bevels, into which were sometimes set tapestries.

The Italian stucco mouldings were also used at that time. The fashion for elaborate ceilings and sidewalls had come to England via Italy and France. The most elaborate ones of those times were executed under Charles II and William III, the ceilings rivalling those of Louis XIV.

William and Mary (1687-1702) brought over with them from Holland, Dutch cabinet makers, which accounts for the marked Dutch influence on the Mahogany Period, an influence which shows in a Dutch style of inlaying, cabriole legs and the tulip design. A sure sign of the William and Mary period is the presence of jasmine, as designed for inlaying in bone, ivory or hollywood.

Lacquer came to England via Holland, the Dutch having imported Chinese workmen.

The entire Mahogany Period, including the Adam brothers, used the shell as a design and the backs of settees resembled several chair backs places side by side.

A feature of the Mahogany Period were the knife-boxes and cases for bottles, made of mahogany and often inlaid, which stood upon pedestals constructed for the purpose, at each side of the sideboard. Later the pedestals became a part of the sideboard. The urn-shaped knife-boxes were extremely graceful as made by Adam, Chippendale and Heppelwhite.

It is impossible to clearly define all of the work of the cabinet-makers of the mahogany or any other period, for reasons already stated. So one must be prepared to find Chippendale sofas which show the shapes originated by him and, also, at times, show Louis XVI legs and Louis XV outline. Chippendale's contemporaries were quite as apt to vary their types, and it is only by experience that one can learn to distinguish between the different artists, to appreciate the hall marks of creative individuality.

The early Chippendale was almost identical with Queen Anne furniture and continued the use of cabriole leg and claw and ball feet. The top of the Chippendale chairs were bow-shaped with ends extending beyond the sides of the back and usually turned up. If turned down they never rounded into the sides, as in the case of Queen Anne chairs. The splats have an upward movement and were joined to chair seats, and not to a cross-rail. They were pierced and showed elaborate ribbon and other designs in carving. There were, also, "ladder backs," and the Chinese Chippendale chairs, with lattice work open carved and extending over entire backs. The characteristic Chippendale leg is cabriole with claw and ball foot.

The setting for Chippendale furniture was a panelled dado, classic mantelpiece, architraves and frieze, and stretched over sidewalks, above dado, was silk or paper showing a large pattern harmonising with the furniture. The Chinese craze brought about a fashion for Chinese wall papers with Chinese designs. This Chinese fashion continued for fifty years.

Chippendale carved the posts of his bedsteads, and so the bed curtains were drawn back and only a short valance was used around the top, whereas in the time of William and Mary bed curtains enveloped all the woodwork. Still earlier in the Elizabethan period bed posts were elaborately carved.

In the eighteenth century it was the fashion to embroider the bed curtains.

The Chippendale china-cabinets with glass fronts, were the outcome of the fad for collecting Chinese and French porcelain, and excellent taste was displayed in collecting these small articles within definite and appropriate limits. Cabinets with glass doors were also used as receptacles for silverware.

Thomas Sheraton (1760-1786), another great name in the Mahogany Period, admired Louis XV and Louis XVI and one can easily trace French influence in the "light, rhythmic style" he originated. Sheraton's contribution to interior decoration was furniture. His rooms, walls, ceilings, over-doors, windows and chimney pieces, are considered very poor; which accounts for the fact that Sheraton furniture as well as Heppelwhite was used in Adam rooms.

Sheraton made a specialty of pieces of furniture designed to serve several purposes, and therefore adapted for use in small rooms; such as dressing-tables with folding mirrors, library step-ladders convertible into tables, etc.

The backs of Sheraton chairs had straight tops and several small splats joined to a cross-rail, and not to the seat. The legs were straight.

Sheraton introduced the use of turned work on the legs and outer supports of the backs of chairs, and produced fine examples of painted furniture, especially painted satin-wood. He, also, did some very fine inlaying and used cane in the seats and backs of chairs which he painted black and gold. Among those who decorated for him was Angelica Kauffman.

Heppelwhite chairs are unmistakable on account of their shield, heart or oval backs and open splats, which were not joined to the seat in the centre of backs. The most beautiful were those with carved Prince of Wales feathers, held together by a bow-knot delicately carved. They were sometimes painted. The legs of Heppelwhite furniture were straight.

We see in the book published by A. Heppelwhite & Co., a curious statement to the effect that cabriole chairs were those having stuffed backs. This idea must have arisen from the fact that many chairs of the eighteenth century with cabriole legs, did have stuffed backs.

Robert Adam, born in 1785, was an architect and decorative artist. The Adam rooms, walls, ceilings, mantels, etc., are the most perfect of the period; beautiful classic mouldings encrust ceilings and sidewalls, forming panels into which were let paintings, while in drawing-rooms the side panels were either recessed so as to hold statuary in the antique style, or were covered with damask or tapestry. It is stated that damask and tapestry were never used on the walls of Adam dining-rooms. James Adam, a brother, worked with Robert.

Every period had its own weak points, so we find the Adam brothers at times making wall-brackets which were too heavy with ram's heads, garlands, etc., and the Adam chairs were undoubtedly bad. They had backs with straight tops, rather like Sheraton chairs, and several small splats joining top rail to seat. The bad chairs by Adam, were improved upon by Sheraton and Heppelwhite. The legs of Adam furniture were straight.

The ideal eighteenth century interior in England was undoubtedly an Adam room with Heppelwhite or Sheraton furniture.

Sir John Soane, architect, had one of the last good house interiors, for the ugly Georgian style came on the scene about 1812. Grinling Gibbons' carvings of heavy fruits and flowers, festoons and masks made to be used architecturally we now see used on furniture, and often heavily gilded.

William Morris was an epoch maker in English interior decoration, for he stood out for the "great, simple note" in furnishings. The pre-Raphaelites worked successfully to the same end, reviving classic simplicity and establishing the value of elimination. The good, modern furniture of to-day, designed with reference to meeting the demands of modern conditions, undoubtedly received a great impetus from that reaction to the simple and harmonious.

CHAPTER XXII

THE COLONIAL PERIOD

The furniture made in America during the eighteenth and early nineteenth centuries was reproduced from English models and shows the influence of Chippendale, Sheraton, Heppelwhite and the Adam brothers. For those interested in these early types of American output, the Sage and other collections in the Metropolitan Museum, New York, give a delightful object lesson, and there has been much written on the subject in case any data is desired.

If some of our readers own heirlooms and plan reproducing Colonial interiors of the finest type, we would advise making an effort to see some of the beautiful New England or Virginia homes, which remain quite as they were in the old days; fine square rooms with hand-carved woodwork, painted white, their walls panelled in wood and painted the same white. Into these panels were set hand-painted wall paper. The authors saw some made for a house in Peabody, near Salem, Massachusetts, some time between 1760 and 1800, and were amazed to find that the colours were as vivid as when first put on.

Here let us say that the study of interior decoration throws a strong light on the history of walls. In Gothic days the stone or wood of the feudal hall was partially concealed by tapestries,—the needlework of the women of the household, a record of the gallant deeds of men used as interior decoration. Later of course, the making of tapestries became a great industry in Italy, France and Belgium, an industry patronised by kings and the nobility, and subsidised by governments.

Next we have walls sheathed with wood panelling. Then during the late Renaissance, painted portraits were let into these panels and became a part of the walls. Later, the upper half, or two-thirds of the panelling, was left off, and only a low panelling, or "dado," remained. This, too, disappeared in time.

Landscape paper was the bridge between the panelled walls with pictures built into them, and the painted or papered walls with pictures hung on them. The paper which we have already referred to, is one of the finest examples of its kind, and while there is only enough for one side of a room, it is valued at $5,000. The design is eight feet high, each strip 22 inches wide, and there are eighteen of the original twenty strips. Two breaks occur, numbers 16 and 18. The owner believes that the Puritan attitude of her ancestors caused them to destroy the panels which showed nude figures engaged in battle. This paper is now the property of Mrs. Eliza Brown of Salem, Massachusetts. It was found in her grandfather's attic in Gloucester, and was given to Mrs. Brown by her grandmother. It was in an army chest belonging to Judutham Baldwin, a Colonel of Engineers in the Revolutionary Army, who laid out the forts in Boston Harbour.

Kate Sanborn, in her book on "Old Wall Papers" speaks of this particular paper. "Paper from the Ham House at Peabody, Massachusetts, now occupied by Dr. Worcester. Shows tropical scenes. These scenes are quite similar to those of the Pizarro paper and may have been the work of the same designer." (The so-called "Pizarro in Peru" paper is shown in plate 34 and 35 of the same book, and is in Duxbury, Mass.) Pizarro's invasion of Peru was in 1531. The colouring of Mrs. Brown's paper is white background with foliage in vivid greens, while figures of Peruvians wear costumes of brilliant blues and vermillion reds, a striking contrast to their soft, brown skins.

This paper is now in the market, but let us hope it may finally rest in a museum.

CHAPTER XXIII

THE REVIVAL OF DIRECTOIRE AND EMPIRE FURNITURE

The revival of Directoire and Empire furniture within the past few years, is attributed by some, to that highly artistic, and altogether illuminating publication, the Gazette do Bon Ton—Arts, Modes and Frivolities—published in Paris by the Librarie Centrale des Beaux Arts, 13 rue Lafayette and contributed to by the leading artists of Paris—the ultra moderns.

There was a time, fifteen or twenty years ago, when one could buy Empire furniture at very low figures, for in those days there was many a chance to pick up such pieces. To-day, a genuine antique or a hand-made reproduction of an antique made sixty years ago, will command a large price, and even in Paris one has difficulty in finding them in the shops at any price.

Empire furniture ceased to be admired in America when the public got "fed up" on this type by its indiscriminate use in hotels and other public buildings.

The best designers of modern painted furniture are partly responsible for the revived interest in both Empire and Directoire. From their reproductions of the beautiful simple outlines, we, as a people, are once more beginning to feel line and to recognise it as an intrinsic part of beauty.

PLATE XXI

A Victorian group in a small portion of a very large parlour, 70 x 40 feet, one of the few remaining, if not the last, of the old Victorian mansions in New York City, very interesting as a specimen of the most elegant style of furnishing in the first half of the nineteenth century.

We would call attention to the heavy moulding of ceilings, the walls painted in panels (painted panels or wall paper to represent panels, is a Victorian hallmark), beautifully hand-carved woodwork, elaboration of design and colon carpet, woven in one piece for the room; in fact the characteristic richness of elaboration everywhere: Pictures in gilded carved frames, hung on double silk cords with tassels, heavily carved furniture made in England, showing fruits, flowers and medallion heads, and a similar elaboration and combination of flora and figures on bronze gas fixtures.

Part of a Victorian Parlour in One of the Few Remaining New York Victorian Mansions

Heavy curtains of satin damask hung at the windows, held back by great cords and tassels, from enormous brass cornices in the form of gigantic flowers.

Also of the period is an immense glass case of stuffed birds, standing in the corner of the large dining-room. This interior was at the height of its glory at the time of the Civil War, and one is told of wonderful parties when the uniforms of the Northern officers decorated the stately rooms and large shaded gardens adjoining the house.

As things go in New York it may be but a matter of months before this picturesque landmark is swept away by relentless Progress.

CHAPTER XXIV

THE VICTORIAN PERIOD

Gradually architecture and interior decoration drew apart, becoming two distinct professions, until during the Victorian era the two were unrelated with the result that the period of Victorian furniture is one of the worst on record.

There were two reasons for this divorce of the arts, which for centuries had been one in origin and spirit; first, the application of steam to machinery (1815) leading to machine-made furniture, and second, the invention of wall-paper which gradually took the place of wood panelling and shut off the architects from all jurisdiction over the decoration of the home.

With the advent of machine-made furniture came cheap imitations of antiques and the rapid decadence of this art. Hand-made reproductions are quite another thing. Sir Richard Wallace (of the Wallace Collection, London) is said to have given $40,000 for a reproduction of the bureau du Louvre.

Fortunately, of late years a tide has set in which favours simple, well made furniture, designed with fine lines and having special reference to the purposes for which each piece is intended, and to-day our houses can be beautiful even if only very simple and inexpensive furniture is used.

In the Victorian prime, even the carved furniture, so much of which was made in England both for that country and the United States (*see Plate XXI*), was not of the finest workmanship, compared with carvings of the same time in Belgium, France, Germany and Austria.

To-day Victorian cross-stitch and bead work in chairs, screens, footstools and bell-pulls, artificial flowers of wax and linen, and stuffed birds, as well as Bristol glass in blue, green and violet, are brought out from their hiding places and serve as touches of colour to give some of the notes of variety which good interior decoration demands.

To be fascinating, a person must not be too rigidly one type. There must be moments of relaxation, of light and shade in mood, or one is not charmed even by great beauty. So your perfect room must not be kept too rigidly in one style. To have attraction it must have variety in both line and colour, and reflect the taste of generations of home lovers. The contents of dusty garrets may add piquancy to modern decorations, giving a touch of the unusual which is very charming.

CHAPTER XXV

PAINTED FURNITURE

Painted furniture is, at present, the vogue, so if you own a piece made by the Adam brothers of England, decorated by the hand of Angelica Kauffman, or Pergolesi, from Greek designs, now is the moment to "star" it.

Different in decoration, but equal in charm, is the seventeenth and eighteenth century painted lacquers of Italy, France, China and Japan. In those days great masters laboured at cabinetmaking and decorating, while distinguished artists carved the woodwork of rooms, and painted the ceilings and walls of even private dwellings.

To-day we have reproductions (good and bad) of the veteran types, and some commendable inventions, more or less classic in line, and original in colouring and style of decoration. At times, one wishes there was less evident effort to be original. We long for the repose of classic colour schemes and classic line. In art, the line and the combination of colours which have continued most popular throughout the ages, are very apt to be those with which one can live longest and not tire. For this reason, a frank copy of an antique piece of painted furniture is generally more satisfactory than a modern original.

If you are using dull coloured carpets and hangings, have your modern reproductions antiqued. If you prefer gay, cheering tones, let the painted furniture be bright. These schemes are equally interesting in different ways. It is stupid to decry new things, since every grey antique had its frivolous, vivid youth.

One American decorator has succeeded in making the stolid, uncompromising squareness of mission furniture take on a certain lightness and charm by painting it black and discreetly lining it with yellow and red. Yellow velour is used for the seat pads and heavy hangings, thin yellow silk curtains are hung at the windows, and the black woodwork is set off by Japanese gold paper. In a large house, or in a summer home where there are young people coming and going, a room decorated in this fashion is both gay and charming and makes a pleasant contrast to darker rooms. Then, too, yellow is a lovely setting for all flowers, the effect being to intensify their beauty, as when flooded by sunshine.

Another clever treatment of the mission type, which we

include under the heading Painted Furniture, is to have it stained a rich dark brown, instead of the usual dark green. Give your dealer time to order your furniture unfinished from the factory, and have stained to your own liking; or, should you by any chance be planning to use mission in one of those cottages so often built in Maine, for summer occupancy, where the walls are of unplastered, unstained, dove-tailed boards, and the floors are unstained and covered with matting rugs, try using this furniture in its natural colour—unfinished. The effect is delightfully harmonious and artistic and quite Japanese in feeling.

In such a cottage, the living-room has a raftered ceiling, the sidewalls, woodwork, settles by the fireplaces, open bookcases and floor, are all stained dark walnut. The floor colour is very dark, the sidewalls, woodwork and book shelves are a trifle lighter, and the ceiling boards still lighter between the almost black, heavy rafters. The mission furniture is dark brown, the hangings and cushions are of mahogany-coloured corduroy, and the floor is strewn with skins of animals. There are no pictures, the idea being to avoid jarring notes in another key. Instead, copper and brass bowls contribute a note of variety, as well as large jars filled with great branches of flowers, gathered in the nearby woods. The chimney is exposed. It and the large open fireplace are of rough, dark mottled brick.

A room of this character would be utterly spoiled by introducing white as ornaments, table covers, window curtains or picture-mats; it is a colour scheme of dull wood-browns, old reds and greens in various tones. If you want your friends' photographs about you in such a room, congregate them on one or two shelves above your books.

CHAPTER XXVI

TREATMENT OF AN INEXPENSIVE BEDROOM

The experience of the author is that the most attractive, inexpensive furniture is that made by the Leavens factory in Boston. This furniture is so popular with all interior decorators that it needs no further advertising. Order for each single iron bed two foot boards, instead of a head and a footboard. This the factory will supply upon demand. Then have your bed painted one of the colours you have chosen as in the colour scheme for your room. Say, the prevailing note of your chintz. Have two rolls made, to use at the head and foot (which are now of equal height) and cover these and the bed with chintz, or, if preferred, with sun-proof material in one of the other colours in your chintz. By this treatment your cheap iron bed of ungainly proportions, has attained the quality of an interesting, as well as unique, "day-bed."

PLATE XXII

Two designs for day-beds which are done in colours to suit the scheme of any room.

These beds are fitted with box springs and a luxurious mattress of feathers or down, covered with silk or chintz, coverlet and cushions of similar material, in colours harmonising with beds. If desired, these lounges can be made higher from the floor.

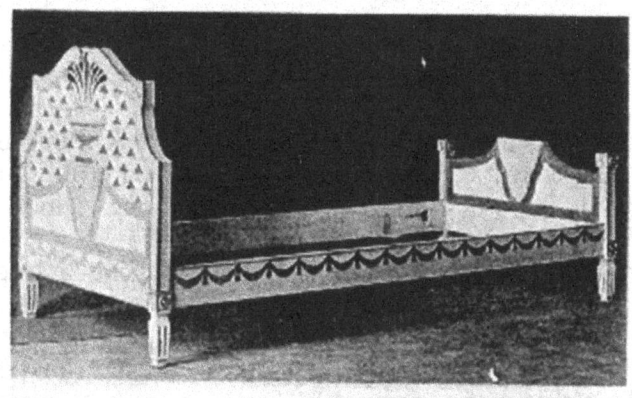

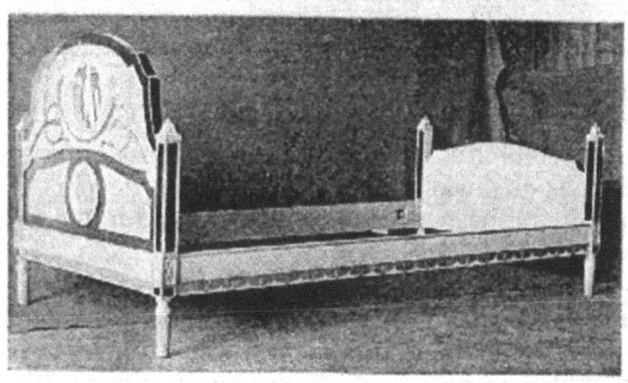

Two Styles of Day-beds

The most attractive cheap bureau is one ordered "in the plain" from the factory, and painted like the bed. If you would entirely remove the factory look, have the mirror taken off the bureau and hang it on the wall over what, by your operation, has become a chest of drawers. If you want a long mirror in your rooms, the cheapest variety is mirror glass, fastened to the back of doors with picture moulding to match woodwork. This is also the cheapest variety of over-mantel mirrors. We have seen it used with great success, let into walls of narrow halls and bedrooms and framed with a dull-gold moulding in the style of room.

For chairs, use the straight wooden ones which are made to match the bureau, and paint them like the bed and bureau.

For comfortable arm-chairs, wicker ones with chintz-covered pads for seat and back are best for the price, and these can also be painted.

Cheap tables, which match the bureau, when painted will do nicely as a small writing-table or a night-table for water, clock, book, etc.

If the floors are new and of hard wood, wax them and use a square of plain velvet carpet in a dark tone of your dominant colour. Or if economy is your aim, use attractive rag rugs which are very cheap and will wash.

If your floors are old and you intend using a large velvet square, paint the edges of the floor white, or some pale shade to match the colour of the walls. Or, use filling all over the floor. If you cannot afford either and must use small rugs, stain or paint your floors a dark colour, to be practical, and use only necessary rugs; that is, one before bed, bureau and fireplace.

Sofas are always expensive. That is one reason for advising that beds be treated like "day-beds."

Wall papers, at ten cents a roll, come in charming colours and designs, and with a few cheap French coloured prints, framed in passepartout, your room is attractive at once.

If your prints are black and white use broad passepartout in same colour as the wall paper, only a tone deeper. If you use favourite photographs, suppress all margins and frame with narrow black passepartout.

For curtains use one of the sixty-or seventy-cent chintzes which come in attractive designs and colours, or what is still cheaper, sun-proof material, fifty inches wide (from $1.10 to $1.50 a yard), and split it in half for curtains, edging them with a narrow fringe of a contrasting colour which appears in the chintz of chair-pads. Another variety of cheap curtains is heavy cream scrim with straps (for looping back) and valance of chintz. These come cheaper than all chintz curtains and are very effective, suggesting the now popular and expensive combination of plain toned taffetas combined with chintz.

Use for sash curtains plain scrim or marquesette.

Let your lamps be made of inexpensive one-toned pottery vases, choosing for these still another colour which appears in the chintz. The lamp shades can be made of a pretty near-silk, in a plain colour, with a fringe made up of one, two or three of the colours in the chintz.

If you happen to have your heart set on deep rose walls and your bedroom furniture is mahogany, find a chintz with rose and French blue, and then cover your arm-chair pads and bed with chintz, but make your curtains of blue sun-proof material, having a narrow fringe of rose, and use a deep rose carpet, or rugs, or if preferred, a dull brown carpet to harmonise with the furniture. A plain red Wilton carpet will dye an artistic deep mulberry brown. They are often bought in the red and dyed to get this shade of brown.

For attractive cheap dining-room furniture, buy simple shapes, unfinished, and have the table, sideboard and chairs painted dark or light, as you prefer.

In your dining-room and halls, if the house is old and floors bad, and economy necessary, use a solid dark linoleum, either deep blue or red, and have it waxed, as an economical measure as well as to improve its appearance.

In a small home, where no great formality is observed, well chosen doilies may be used on all occasions, instead of table cloths. By this expedient you suppress one large item on the laundry bill, the care of the doilies in such cases falling to the waitress.

To make comfortable, convenient and therefore livable, a part of a house, formerly an attic, or an extension with small rooms and low ceilings, seems to be the special province of a certain type of mind, which works best when there is a tax on the imagination.

When reclaiming attic rooms, one of the problems is how to get wall space, especially if there are dormer windows and very slanting ceilings. One way, is to place a dressing table in the dormer, under windows, covering the sides of the dormer recess with mirror glass, edged with narrow moulding. The dressing-table is not stationary, therefore it can be easily moved by a maid, when the rooms are cleaned.

CHAPTER XXVII

TREATMENT OF A GUEST ROOM

(Where economy is not an item of importance)

Here we can indulge our tastes for beautiful quality of materials and fine workmanship, as well as good line and colour, so we describe a room which has elegant distinction and atmosphere, yet is not a so-called period room—rather a modern room, in the sense that it combines beautiful lines and exquisite colouring with every modern development for genuine comfort and convenience.

The walls are panelled and painted a soft taupe—there are no pictures; simply one very beautiful mirror in a dull-gold frame, a Louis XVI reproduction.

PLATE XXIII

In another suite we have a boudoir done in sage greens and soft browns. The curtains of taffeta, in stripes of the two colours. Two tiers of creme net form sash curtains.

The carpet is a rich mulberry brown, day-bed a reproduction of an antique, painted in faded greens with panier fleuri design on back, in lovely faded colours, taffeta cushions of sage green and an occasional note about the room of mulberry and dull blue. Electric light shades are of decorated parchment paper.

Really an enchanting nest, and as it is in a New York apartment, and occasionally used as a bedroom, a piece of furniture has been designed for it similar to the wardrobe shown in picture, only not so high. The glass door, when open, disclose a toilet table, completely fitted out, the presence of which one would never suspect.

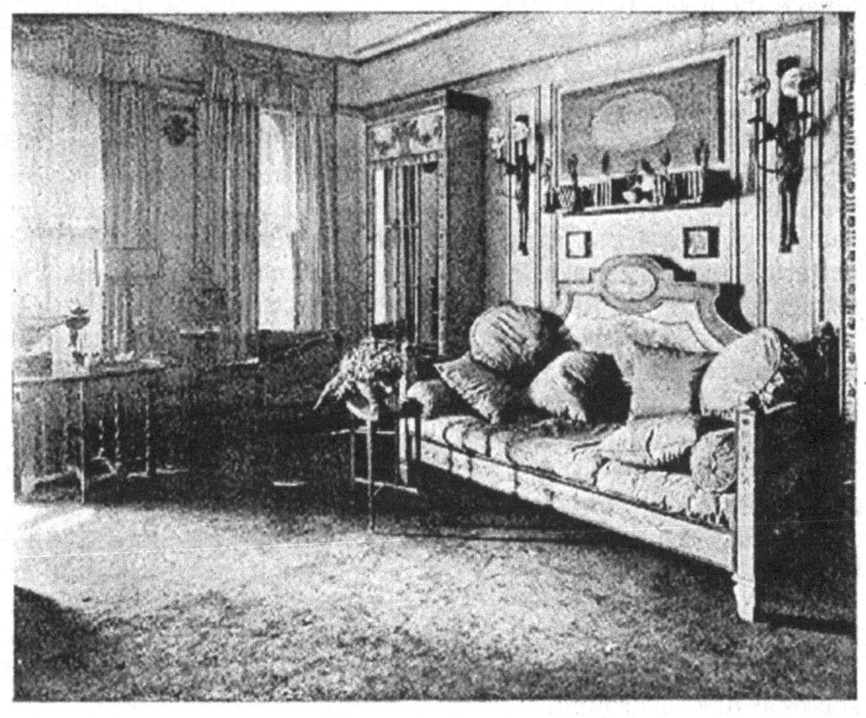

Boudoir in New York Apartment. Painted Furniture, Antique and Reproductions.

The carpet made of dark taupe velvet covers the entire floor. The furniture is Louis XV, of the wonderful painted sort, the beautiful bed with its low head and foot boards exactly the same height, curving backward; the edges a waved line, the ground-colour a lovely pistache green, and the decoration gay old-fashioned garden flowers in every possible shade. The bureau has three or four drawers and a bowed front with clambering flowers. These two pieces, and a delightful night-table are exact copies of the Clyde Fitch set in the Cooper Hewitt Museum, at New York; the originals are genuine antiques, and their colour soft from age.

A graceful dressing-table, with winged mirrors, has been designed to go with this set, and is painted like the bureau. The glass is a modern reproduction of the lovely old eighteenth century mirror glass which has designs cut into it, forming a frame.

For chairs, all-over upholstered ones are used, of good lines and proportions; two or three for comfort, and a low slipper-chair for convenience. These are covered in a chintz with a light green ground, like the furniture, and flowered in roses and violets, green foliage and lovely blue sprays.

The window curtains are of soft, apple-green taffeta, trimmed with a broad puffing of the same silk, edged on each side by black moss-trimming, two inches wide. These curtains hang from dull-gold cornices of wood, with open carving, through which one gets glimpses of the green taffeta of the curtains.

The sash-curtains are of the very finest cream net, and the window shades are of glazed linen, a deep cream ground, with a pattern showing a green lattice over which climb pink roses. The shades are edged at the bottom with a narrow pink fringe.

The bed has a cover of green taffeta exactly like curtains, with the same trimming of puffed taffeta, edged with a black moss-trimming.

The mantelpiece is true to artistic standards and realises the responsibility of its position as keynote to the room. Placed upon it are a beautiful old clock and two vases, correct as to line and colour.

Always be careful not to spoil a beautiful mantel or beautiful ornaments by having them out of proportion one with the other. Plate XXIV shows a mantel which fails as a composition because the bust, an original by Behnes, beautiful in itself, is too heavy for the mantel it stands on and too large for the mirror which reflects it and serves as its background.

Keep everything in correct proportion to the whole. We have in mind the instance of some rarely beautiful walls taken from an ancient monastery in Parma, Italy. They were ideal in their original setting, but since they have been transported to America, no setting seems right. They belonged in a building where there were a succession of small rooms with low ceilings, each room perfect like so many pearls on a string. Here in America their only suitable place would be a museum, or to frame the tiny "devotional" of some précieuse Flower of Modernity.

CHAPTER XXVIII

A MODERN HOUSE IN WHICH GENUINE JACOBEAN FURNITURE IS APPROPRIATELY SET

An original scheme for a dining-room was recently carried out in a country house in England by a woman whose hobby is illuminating. It will appeal to experts in the advance guard of interior decoration. The woman in question was stimulated for her task by coming into possession of some interesting Jacobean pieces of furniture, of oak, squarely and solidly made, with flat carvings, characteristic of the period.

PLATE XXIV

A beautiful mantel, a beautiful mirror, beautiful ornaments, and a rare and beautiful marble bust by Behnes, but because the bust is too large for both mantel and reflecting mirror, the composition is poor.

Example of Lack of Balance in Mantel Arrangement

The large Jacobean chest happened to be lined, as many of those old chests were, with quaint figured paper, showing a coat-of-arms alternating with another design in large squares of black and grey. This paper, the owner had reproduced to cover the walls of her dining-room, and then she stained her woodwork black (giving the effect of old black oak), also, the four corner cupboards, but the inside of these cupboards—doors and all—she made a rich Pompeian red and lackered it. The doors are left open and one sees on the shelves of the corner cupboards a wonderful collection of old china, much of it done in rich gold. At night the whole is illuminated with invisible electric bulbs. The gleaming effect is quite marvellous.

The seat-pads on chairs, are made of hides, gilded all over, and on the gilt the owner has painted large baskets holding fruit and flowers done in gay colours. The long Jacobean bench has a golden cushion with baskets painted on it in gay colours.

A part of the wonderful gold china is used at every meal, and the rest of it being left on the shelves of the four cupboards with their Pompeian red lining, when lit up, forms part of the glowing blaze of colour, concentrated in all four corners of this unique room.

The Jacobean library in this house has the same black oak effect for panelling and at the windows, hang long, red silk curtains, with deep borders of gold on which are painted gay flowers. This blaze of colour is truly Jacobean and recalls the bedroom at Knole, occupied by James I where the bed-curtains were of red silk embroidered in gorgeous gold, and the high post bedstead heavily carved, covered with gold and silver tissue, lined with red silk, its head-board carved and gilded.

Another room at Knole was known as the "Spangle" bedroom. James I gave the furniture in it to Lionel, Earl of Middlesex. Bed curtains, as well as the seats of chairs and stools, are of crimson, heavily embroidered in gold and silver.

CHAPTER XXIX

UNCONVENTIONAL BREAKFAST-ROOMS AND SPORTS BALCONIES

"Sun-rooms" are now a feature of country and some town houses. One of the first we remember was in Madrid, at the home of Canovas del Castillo, Prime Minister during the Regency. Déjeuner used to be served at one end of the conservatory, in the shadow of tall palms, while fountains played, birds with gay plumage sang, and the air was as fragrant as the tropics. For comfort, deep red rugs were put down on the white marble floors. Which reminds us that in many Spanish hand-made rugs, what is known as "Isabella white" figures conspicuously. The term arises from the following story. It seems that Queen Isabella during the progress of some war, vowed she would not have her linen washed until her army returned victorious. The war was long, hence the term!

In furnishing a conservatory or porch breakfast room, it is best to use some variety of informal tables and chairs, such as painted furniture, willow or bamboo, and coloured, not white, table cloths, doilies and napkins, to avoid the glare from the reflection of strong light. Also, informal china, glass, etc.

Screens, if necessary, should have frames to accord with the furniture, and the panels should be of wood, or some simple material such as sacking or rough linen, which comes in lovely vivid, out-of-door colours.

The bizarre and fascinating sports balconies overlooking squash courts, tennis courts, golf links, croquet grounds, etc., are among the newest inventions of the decorator. Furnished porches we have all grown accustomed to, and when made so as to be enclosed by glass, in inclement weather, they may be treated like inside rooms in the way of comforts and conveniences.

The smart porch-room is furnished with only such chairs, tables, sofas and rugs as are appropriate to a place not thoroughly protected from the elements, for while glass is provided for protection, a summer shower can outstrip a slow-footed servant and valuable articles made for indoors cannot long brave the effect of rain and hot sun.

PLATE XXV

In this case the house stood so near the road that there was no privacy, so the ingenious architect-decorator became landscape-gardener and by making a high but ornamental fence and numerous arbours, carried the eye to the green trees beyond and back to the refreshing tangle of shrubs and flowers in the immediate foreground, until the illusion of being secluded was so complete that the nearby road was forgotten.

Treatment of Ground Lying Between House and Much Travelled Country Road

For this reason furnish your porch with colours which do not fade, and with wicker furniture which knows how to contract and expand to order!

The same rule applies to rugs. Put your Oriental rugs indoors, and use inexpensive, effective porch rugs which, with a light heart, you can renew each season, if necessary.

The sports balcony is fitted out with special reference to the comfort of those who figure as audience for sports, and as a lounge between games, and each hostess vies with her friends in the originality and completeness of equipment, as well as in the costumes she dons in her commendable desire to make of herself a part of her scheme of decoration.

A country place which affords tennis courts, golf links, cricket and polo grounds or has made arrangements for the exercise of any sports, usually makes special provision for the comfort of those engaging in them, more or less as a country club does. There is a large porch for lounging and tea, and a kitchenette where tea, cooling drinks and sandwiches are easily and quickly prepared, without interfering with the routine of the kitchens. There are hot and cold plunge baths, showers, a swimming pool, dressing rooms with every convenience known to man or woman, and a room given over to racks which hold implements used in the various sports, as well as lockers for sweaters, change of linen, socks, etc., belonging to those stopping in the house.

Where sports are a main issue, an entire building is often devoted to the comfort of the participants. We have in mind the commodious and exceptionally delightful arrangements made for the comfort and pleasure of those playing court tennis in a large and architecturally fine building erected for the purpose on the estate of the Neville Lyttons, Crabber Park, Poundhill, England.

If sport balconies overlook tennis courts or golf links, they are fitted out with light-weight, easily moved, stiff chairs for the audience, and easy, cushioned arm-chairs and sofas of upholstered wicker, for the participants to lounge in between matches.

Card tables are provided, as well as small tea tables, to seat two, three or four, while there is always one oblong table at which a sociable crowd of young people may gather for chatter and tea!

If you use rail-boxes, or window-boxes, holding growing plants, be sure that the flowers are harmonious in colour when seen from the lawn, road or street, against their background of house and the awnings and chintzes, used on the porch.

The flowers in window-boxes and on porch-rails must first of all decorate the outside of your house. Therefore, before you buy your chintz for porches, decide as to whether the colour of your house, and its awnings, demands red, pink, white, blue, yellow or mauve flowers, and then choose your chintz and porch rugs as well as porch table-linen, to harmonise.

In selecting porch chairs remember that women want the backs of most of the chairs only as high as their shoulders, on account of wearing hats.

CHAPTER XXX

SUN-ROOMS

There are countless fascinating schemes for arranging sun-rooms. One which we have recently seen near Philadelphia, was the result of enclosing a large piazza, projecting from an immense house situated in the midst of lawns and groves.

The walls are painted orange and striped with pale yellow; the floors are covered with the new variety of matting which imitates tiles, and shows large squares of colour, blocked off by black. The chintzes used are in vivid orange, yellow and green, in a stunning design; the wicker chairs are painted orange and black, and from the immense iridescent globes of electric light hang long, orange silk tassels.

PLATE XXVI

Shows how to utilise and make really very attractive an extension roof, by converting it into a balcony.

An awning of broad green and white stripes protect this one in winter as well as summer, and by using artificial ivy, made of tin and painted to exactly imitate nature, one gets, as you see, a charming effect.

An Extension Roof in New York Converted into a Balcony

Iron fountains, wonderful designs in black and gold, throw water over gold and silver fish, or gay water plants; while, in black and gold cages, vivid parrots and orange-coloured canaries gleam through the bars. Iron vases of black and gold on tall pedestals, are filled with trailing ivy and bright coloured plants. Along the walls are wicker sofas, painted orange and black, luxuriously comfortable with down cushions covered, as are some of the chair cushions, in soft lemon, sun-proofed twills.

Here one finds card-tables, tea-tables and smoking-tables, a writing-desk fully equipped, and at one end, a wardrobe of black and gold, hung with an assortment of silk wraps and "wooleys"—for an unprovided and chilly guest, in early spring, when the steam heat is off and the glass front open.

Even on a grey, winter day, this orange and gold room seems flooded with sun, and gives one a distinctly cheerful sensation when entering it from the house.

Of course, if your porch-room is mainly for mid-summer use and your house in a warm region, then we commend instead of sun-producing colours, cool tones of green, grey or blue. If your porch floor is bad, cover it with dark-red linoleum and wax it. The effect is like a cool, tiled floor. On this you can use a few porch rugs.

Black and white awnings or awnings in broad, green-and-white stripes, or plain green awnings, are deliciously cool-looking, and rail-boxes filled with green and white or blue and pale pink flowers are refreshing on a summer day.

By the sea, where the air is bracing, and it is not necessary to trick the senses with a pretence at coolness, nothing is more satisfactory or gay than scarlet geraniums; but if they are used, care must be taken that they harmonise with the colour of the awnings and the chintz on the porch.

Speaking of rail-boxes reminds us that in making over a small summer house and converting a cheap affair into one of some pretensions, remember that one of the most telling points is the character of your porch railing. So at once remove the cheap one with its small, upright slats and the insignificant and frail top rail, and have a solid porch railing (or porch fence) built with broad, top rail. Then place all around porch, resting on iron brackets, rail-flower boxes, the tops of these level with the top of the rail, and paint the boxes the colour of the house trimmings. Filled with running vines and gay flowers, nothing could be more charming.

Window-boxes make any house lovely and are a large part of that charm which appeals to us, whether the house be a mansion in Mayfair or a Bavarian farm house. Americans are learning this.

The window and rail-boxes of a house look best when all are planted with the same variety of flowers.

Having given a certain air of distinction to your porch-railing, add another touch to the appearance of your small, remodelled house by having the shutters hung from the top of the windows, instead of from the sides. A charming variety of awning or sunshades, to keep the sun and glare out of rooms, is the old English idea of a straw-thatching, woven in and out until it makes a broad, long mat which is suspended from the top of windows, on the outside of the house, being held out and permanently in place, at the customary angle of awnings. We first saw this picturesque kind of rustic awnings used on little cottages of a large estate in Vermont, cottages once owned and lived in by labourers, but bought and put in comfortable condition to be used as overflow rooms for guests, in connection with the large family mansion (once the picturesque village inn).

The art of making these straw awnings is not generally understood in America. In the case to which we refer, one of the gardeners employed on the estate, chanced to be an old Englishman who had woven the straw window awnings for farm houses in his own country.

The straw awnings, with window-boxes planted with bright geraniums and vines, make an inland cottage delightfully picturesque and are practical, although by the sea the straw awnings might be destroyed by high winds.

CHAPTER XXXI

TREATMENT OF A WOMAN'S DRESSING-ROOM

Every house, or flat, which is at all pretentious, should arrange a Vanity Room for the use of guests, in which there are full-length mirrors, a completely equipped dressing-table with every conceivable article to assist a lady in making her toilet, slipper-chairs and chairs to rest in, and a completely equipped lavatory adjoining.

The woman who takes her personal appearance seriously, just as any artist takes her art (and when dressing is not an art it is not worth discussion) can have her dressing-room so arranged with mirrors, black walls and strong, cleverly reflected, electric lights, that she stands out with a cleancut outline, like a cameo, the minutest detail of her toilet disclosed. With such a dressing-room, it is quite impossible to suffer at the hands of a careless maid, and one can use the black walls as a background for vivid chair covers, sofa cushions and lamp shades.

Off this dressing-room should be another, given over to clothes, with closets equipped with hooks and shelves, glass cabinets for shoes and slippers, and the "show-case" for jewels to be placed in by the maid that the owner may make her selection.

At the time of the Louis, knights and courtiers had large rooms devoted to the care and display of their wardrobes, and even to-day there are men who are serious connoisseurs in the art of clothes.

PLATE XXVII

Interior decoration not infrequently leads to a desire to chic the appearance of one's "out-of-doors." We give an example of a perfectly commonplace barn made interesting by adding green latticework, a small iron balcony, ornamental gate and setting out a few decorative evergreens. Behold a transformation!

A commonplace Barn Made Interesting

The dressing-table should be constructed of material in harmony with the rest of your furniture. It may be of mahogany, walnut, rose wood, satin wood, or some painted variety, or, as is the fashion now, made of silk,—a seventeenth and eighteenth century style (in vogue during the time of the Louis). These are made of taffeta with lace covers on top, and in outline are exactly like the simple dotted-swiss dressing-tables with which every one is familiar,—the usual variety, so easily made by placing a wooden packing box on its side. In this case have your carpenter put shelves inside for boots, shoes and slippers. The entire top is covered with felt or flannel, over which is stretched silk or sateen, in any colour which may harmonise with the room. A flounce, as deep as the box is high, is made of the same material as the top, and tacked to the edges of the table-top. Cover the whole with dotted or plain swiss. A piece of glass, cut to exactly fit the top of the table, is a practical precaution. A large mirror, hung above yet resting on the table, is canopied in the old style, with the same material with which you cover your dressing-table.

If the table is made of the beautiful taffeta, now so popular for this purpose, as well as for curtains, it is, of course, not covered with swiss or lace, except the top, on which is used a fine, hand-made cover, of real lace and hand embroidery, in soft creams,—cream from age, or a judicious bath in weak tea. The glass top laid over this cover protects the lace.

If the table has drawers, each can be neatly covered with the taffeta, as can the frame of any table. A good, up-to-date cabinet-maker understands this work as so much of it is now done.

CHAPTER XXXII

THE TREATMENT OF CLOSETS

The modern architect turns out his closets so complete as to comfort and convenience, that he leaves but little to be done by the professional or amateur decorator. Each perfectly equipped bedroom suite calls for, at least, two closets: one supplied with hooks, padded hangers for coats, and covered hangers for skirts, if the closet is for a woman; or, if it is for a man, with such special requirements as he may desire. In the case of a woman's suite, one closet should consist entirely of shelves. Paint all the closets to harmonise with the suite, and let the paint on the shelves have a second coat of enamel, so that they may be easily wiped off. Supply your shelves with large and small boxes for hats, blouses, laces, veils, etc., neatly covered with paper, or chintz, to harmonise with the room.

Those who dislike too many mirrors in a room may have full length mirrors on the inside of the closet doors.

Either devote certain shelves to your boots, shoes and slippers, or have a separate shallow closet for these-shallow because it is most convenient to have but one row on a shelf.

Where economy is not an item of importance, see that electric lights are placed in all the closets, which are turned on with the action of opening the door.

The elaboration of closets, those with drawers of all sizes and depths, cedar closets for furs, etc., is merely a matter of the architect's planning to meet the specific needs of the occupants of any house.

CHAPTER XXXIII

TREATMENT OF A NARROW HALL

A long, narrow hall in a house, or apartment, is difficult to arrange, but there are methods of treating them which partially corrects their defects. One method is shown on Plate XIV.

The best furnishing is a very narrow console (table) with a stiff, high-backed chair on either side of it, and on the wall, over console, a tapestry, an architectural picture or a family portrait. On the console is placed merely a silver card tray.

Have a closet for wraps if possible, or arrange hooks and a table, out of right, for this purpose. Keep your walls and woodwork light in colour and in the same tone.

PLATE XXVIII

An idea for treatment of a narrow hall, where the practical and beautiful are combined. The hall table and candlesticks are an example of the renaissance of iron, elaborately wrought after classic designs.

The mirror over table is framed in green glass, the ornaments are of dull gold (iron gilded).

The Venetian glass jar is in opalescent green, made to hold dried rose leaves, and used here purely as an ornament which catches and reflects the light, important, as the hall is dark.

The iron of table is black touched with gold, and the marble slab dark-green veined with white.

Narrow Entrance Hall of a New York Antique Shop

An interesting treatment of a long narrow hall is to break its length with lattice work, which has an open arch, wide enough for one or two people to pass through, the arch surmounted by an urn in which ivy is planted. The lattice work has lines running up and down—not crossed, as is the usual way. It is on hinges so that trunks or furniture may be carried through the hall, if necessary. The whole is kept in the same colour scheme as the hall.

CHAPTER XXXIV

TREATMENT OF A VERY SHADED LIVING-ROOM

By introducing plenty of yellow and orange you can bring sunshine into a dark living-room. If your house is in a part of the country where the heat is great, a dark living-room in summer is sometimes a distinct advantage, so keep the colourings subdued in tone, and, therefore, cool looking. If, on the contrary, the living-room is in a cool house on the ocean, or a shaded mountainside, and the sun is cut off by broad porches, you will cheer up your room, and immensely improve it, by using sun-producing colours in chintzes and silks; while cut flowers or growing plants, which reproduce the same colouring, will intensify the illusion of sunshine.

Sash curtains of thin silk, in bright yellows, are always sun-producing, but if you intend using yellows in a room, be careful to do so in combination with browns, greens, greys, or carefully chosen blues, not with reds or magentas.

Try not to mix warm and cold colours when planning your walls. Grey walls call for dull blue or green curtains; white walls for red or green curtains; cream walls for yellow, brown buff or apple green curtains. If your room is too cold, warm it up by making your accessories, such as lamp shades, and sofa pillows, of rose or yellow material.

CHAPTER XXXV

SERVANTS' ROOMS

Whether you expect to arrange for one servant or a dozen, keep in mind the fact that efficiency is dependent upon the conditions under which your manor maid-servant rests as well as works, and that it is as important that the bedroom be attractive as that it be comfortable.

For servants' rooms it is advised that the matter of furnishing and decorating be a scheme which includes comfort, daintiness and effectiveness on the simplest, least expensive basis, no matter how elaborate the house. There is a moral principle involved here. In the case of more than one servant the colour scheme alone needs to be varied, for similar furniture will prevent jealousy among the servants, while at the same time the task of inventing is reduced to the mere multiplying of one room; even the wall paper and chintz being alike in pattern, if different in colour.

The simplest iron beds, or wooden furniture can be painted white or any colour which may be considered more durable.

In maids' rooms for summer use, a vase provided for flowers is sometimes an incentive to personally contribute a touch of beauty. That sense of beauty once awakened in a maid does far more than any words on the subject of order and daintiness in her own room or in those of her employer.

CHAPTER XXXVI

TABLE DECORATION

For the young and inexperienced we state a few rules for table decoration. If you have furnished your dining-room to accord not only with your taste, but the scale upon which you intend living, be careful that the dining-table never strikes a false note, never "gets out of the picture" by becoming too important as to setting or menu. You may live very formally in your town house and very simply, without any ostentation, in the country, but be sure that in all of your experimenting with table decoration you observe above all the law of appropriateness.

Your decoration, flowers, fruit, character of bowl or dish which holds them, or objet d'art used in place of either; linen or lace, china, glass and silver,—each and all must be in keeping. The money value has nothing whatever to do with this question of appropriateness, when considered by an artist decorator. Remember that in decorating, things are classified according to their colour value, their lines and the purpose for which they are intended. The dining-table is to eat at, therefore it should primarily hold only such things as are required for the serving of the meal. So your real decoration should be your silver, glass and china, with its background of linen or lace. The central decoration, if of flowers or fruit, must be in a bowl or dish decorative in the same sense that the rest of the tableware is.

Flowers should be kept in the same key as your room. One may do this and yet have infinite variety. Tall stately lilies, American Beauty roses, great bowls of gardenias and orchids are for stately rooms. Your small house, flat or bungalow require modest garden flowers such as daffodils, jonquils, tulips, lilies-of-the-valley, snapdragons, one long-stemmed rose in a vase, or a cluster of shy moss-buds or nodding tea-roses.

A table set with art in the key of a small menage and on a scale of simple living, often strikes the note of perfection from the expert's point of view because perfect of its kind and suitable for the occasion. This appropriateness is what makes your "smart" table quite as it makes your "smart" woman.

Wedgwood cream colour ware "C.C." is beautiful and always good form. For those wanting colour, the same famous makers of England have an infinite variety, showing lovely designs.

Unless you are a collector in the museum sense, press into service all of your beautiful possessions. If you have to go without them, let it be when you no longer own them, and not because they are hoarded out of sight. You know the story of the man who bought a barrel of apples and each day carefully selected and ate those that were rotten, feeling the necessity of not being wasteful. When the barrel was empty he realised that be had deliberately wasted all his good apples by not eating one! Let this be a warning to him who would save his treasures. If you love antiques and have joyously hunted them down and, perhaps, denied yourself other things to obtain them, you are the person to use them, even though the joy be transient and they perish at the hand of a careless man or maid-servant. Remember, posterity will have its own "fads" and prefer adding the pleasure of pursuit to that of mere ownership. So bring out your treasures and use them!

As there are many kinds of dining-rooms, each good if planned and worked out with an art instinct, so there are many kinds of tables. The usual sort is the round, or square, extension table, laid with fine damask and set with conventional china, glass and silver, rare in quality and distinguished in design. For those who prefer the unusual there are oblong, squarely built Jacobean and Italian refectory tables. With these one makes a point of showing the rich colour of the time-worn wood and carving, for the old Italian tables often have the bevelled edge and legs carved. When this style of table is used, the wood instead of a cloth, is our background, and a "runner" with doilies of old Italian lace takes the place of linen.

In Feudal Days, when an entire household, master and retainers, sat in the baronial hall "above and below the salt," tables were made of great length. When used out of their original setting, they must be cut down to suit modern conditions. In Krakau, Poland, the writer often dined at one of these feudal boards which had been in our hostess's family for several hundred years. To get it into her dining-room a large piece had been cut out at the centre and the two ends pushed together.

For those who live informally, delightfully decorative china can be had at low prices. It was once made only for the peasants, and comes to us from Italy, France, Germany and England. This fact reminds us that when we were travelling in Southern Hungary and were asked to dine with a Magyar farmer, out on the windy Pasta, instead of their usual highly coloured pottery, gay with crude, but decorative flowers, they honoured us by covering the table with American ironstone china! The Hungarian crockery resembles the

Brittany and Italian ware, and some of it is most attractive when rightly set.

When once the passion to depart from beaten paths seizes us it is very easy to make mistakes. Therefore to the housekeeper, accustomed to conventional china, but weary of it, we would commend as a safe departure, modern Wedgwood and Italian reproductions of classic models, which come in exquisite shapes and in a delicious soft cream tone. If one prefers, it is possible to get these varieties decorated with charming designs in artistic colourings, as previously stated.

For eating meals out of doors, or in "sun-rooms," where the light is strong, the dark peasant pottery, like Brittany, Italian and Hungarian, is very effective on dull-blue linen, heavy cream linen or coarse lace, such as the peasants make.

Copper lustre, with its dark metallic surface; is enchanting on dark wood or coloured linen of the right tone.

Your table must be a picture composed on artistic lines. That is, it must combine harmony of line and colour and above all, appropriateness. Gradually one acquires skill in inventing unusual effects; but only the adept can go against established rules of art and yet produce a pleasing ensemble. We can all recall exceptions to this rule for simplicity, beautiful, artistic tables, covered with rare and entrancing objects,—irrelevant, but delighting the eye. Some will instantly recall Clyde Fitch's dinners in this connection, but here let us emphasise the dictum that for a great master of the art of decoration there need be no laws.

A careful study of the Japanese principles of decoration is an ideal way of learning the art of simplicity. It is impossible to deny the immense decorative value of a single objet d'art, as one flower in a simple vase, provided it is given the correct background.

Background in decoration is like a pedal-point in music; it must support the whole fabric, whether you are planning a house, a room or a table.

PLATE XXIX

Shows how a too pronounced rug which is out of character, though a valuable Chinese antique, can destroy the harmony of a composition even where the stage is set with treasures; Louis XV chairs, antique fount with growing plants, candelabra, rare tapestry, reflected by mirror, and a graceful console and a settee with grey-green brocade cushions.

Example of a Charming Hall Spoiled by Too Pronounced a Rug

CHAPTER XXXVII

WHAT TO AVOID IN INTERIOR DECORATION: RULES FOR BEGINNERS

We all know the saying that it is only those who have mastered the steps in dancing who can afford to forget them. It is the same in every art. Therefore let us state at once, that all rules may be broken by the educated—the masters of their respective arts. For beginners we give the following rules as a guide, until they get their bearings in this fascinating game of making pictures by manipulating lines and colours, as expressed in necessary furnishings.

Avoid crowding your rooms, walls or tables, for in creating a home one must produce the quality of restfulness by order and space.

As to walls, do not use a cold colour in a north or shaded room. Make your ceilings lighter in tone than the side walls, using a very pale shade of the same colour as the side walls.

Do not put a spotted (figured) surface on other spotted (figured) surfaces. A plain wall paper is the proper, because most effective, background for pictures.

Avoid the mistake of forgetting that table decoration includes all china, glass, silver and linen used in serving any meal.

In attempting the decoration of your dining-room table avoid anything inappropriate to the particular meal to be served and the scale of service. Do not have too many flowers on your table, or flowers not in harmony with the rest of the setting, in variety or colour.

Do not use peasant china, no matter how decorative in itself, on fine damask or rare lace. By so doing you strike a false note. The background it demands is crash or peasant laces.

Avoid crowding your dining-table or giving it an air of confusion by the number of things on it, thus destroying the laws of simplicity, line and balance in decoration.

Avoid using on your walls as mere decorations articles such as rugs or priests' vestments primarily intended for other purposes.

Avoid the misuse of anything in furnishing. It needs only knowledge and patience to find the correct thing for each need. Better do without than employ a makeshift in decorating.

Inappropriateness and elaboration can defeat artistic beauty—but intelligent elimination never can.

Beware of having about too many vases, or china meant for domestic use. The proper place for table china, no matter how rare it is, is in the dining-room. If very valuable, one can keep it in cabinets.

Useless bric-à-brac in a dining-room looks worse than it does anywhere else.

Your dining-room is the best place for any brasses, copper or pewter you may own.

If sitting-room and dining-room connect by a wide opening, keep the same colour scheme in both, or, in any case, the same depth of colour. This gives an effect of space. It is not uncommon when a house is very small, to keep all of the walls and woodwork, and all of the carpets, in exactly the same colour and tone. If variety in the colour-scheme is desired, it may be introduced by means of cretonnes or silks used for hangings and furniture covers.

Avoid the use of thin, old silks on sofas or chair seats.

Avoid too cheap materials for curtains or chair covers, as they will surely fade.

Avoid too many small rugs in a room. This gives an impression of restless disorder and interferes with the architect's lines. Do not place your rugs at strange angles; but let them follow the lines of the walls.

Avoid placing ornaments or photographs on a piano which is in sufficiently good condition to be used.

Avoid the chance of ludicrous effects. For example, keep a plain background behind your piano. Make sure that, when listening to music you are not distracted by seeing a bewildering section of a picture above the pianist's head, or a silly little vase dodging, as he moves, in front of, above, or below his nose!

Avoid placing vases, or a clock, against a chimney piece already elaborately decorated by the architect, as a part of his scheme in using the moulding of panel to frame a painting over the mantel. In the old palaces one sees that a bit of undecorated background is provided between mantel and the architect's decoration.

If your room has a long wall space, furnish it with a large cabinet or console, or a sofa and two chairs.

Avoid blotting out your architect's cleverest points by thoughtlessly misplacing hangings. Whoever decorates should always keep the architect's intention in mind.

Avoid having an antique clock which does not go, and is used merely as an ornament. Make your rooms alive by having all the clocks running. This is one of the subtleties which marks the difference between an antique shop, or museum, and a home.

Avoid the desecration of the few good antiques you own, by the use of a too modern colour scheme. Have the necessary modern pieces you have bought to supplement your treasures, stained or painted a dull dark colour in harmony with the antiques, and then use dull colours in the floor coverings, curtains and cushions. If you have no good old ornaments, try to get a few good shapes and colours in inexpensive reproductions of the period to which your antiques belong. Avoid the mistake of forgetting that every room is a "stage setting," and must be a becoming and harmonious background for its occupants.

Avoid arranging a Louis XVI bedroom, with fragile antiques and delicate tones, for your husband of athletic proportions and elemental tastes. He will not only feel, but look out of place. If he happens to be fond of artistic things, give him these in durable shades and shapes.

Avoid the omission of a thoroughly masculine sitting-room, library, smoking-room or billiard-room for the man, or men, of the house.

Avoid the use of white linen when eating out of doors. Saxe-blue, red or taupe linen are restful to the eyes. In fact, after one has used coloured linen, white seems glaring and unsympathetic even indoors, and one instinctively chooses the old deep-cream laces. Granting this to be a bit précieuse, we must admit that the traditional white damask, under crystal and silver, or gold plate with rare porcelains, has its place and its distinction in certain houses, and with certain people.

PLATE XXX

Shows a man's library, masculine gender written all over it-strength, comfort, usefulness and simplicity.

The mantel is arranged in accordance with rules already stated. It will be noticed that the ornaments on mantel in a way interfere with design of the large architectural picture.

A Man's Library

Avoid in a studio, bungalow or a small flat, where the living-room and dining-room are the same, all evidences of dining-room (china, silver and glass for use). Let the table be covered with a piece of old or modern brocade when not set for use. A lamp and books further emphasises the note of living-room.

Avoid the use of light-absorbing colours in wall papers if you are anxious to create sympathetic cheerfulness in your rooms, and an appearance of winning comfort. Almost all dark colours are light-absorbing; greens, dull reds, dark greys and mahogany browns will make a room dull in character no matter how much sunlight comes in, or how many electric lights you use. Perhaps the only dark colour which is not light-absorbing is a dark yellow.

Avoid the permanent tea-table. We are glad to record that one seldom happens upon one, these days. How the English used to revile them! In the simplest homes it is always possible at the tea hour, to have a table placed before whoever is to "pour" and a tray on which are cups, tea, cream, sugar, lemon, toast, cake or what you will, brought in from the pantry or kitchen. There was a time when in America, one shuddered at the possibility of dusty cups and those countless faults of a seldom-rehearsed tea-table!

Avoid serving a lunch in an artificially lighted room. This, like a permanent tea-table, is an almost extinct fashion. Neither was sensible, because inappropriate, and therefore bad form. The only possible reason for shutting out God's sunlight and using artificial lights, is when the function is to begin by daylight and continue until after nightfall.

If in doubt as to what is good, go often to museums and compare what you own, or have seen and think of owning, with objects in museum collections.

CHAPTER XXXVIII

FADS IN COLLECTING

In a New York home one room is devoted to a so-called panier fleuri collection which in this case means that each article shows the design of a basket holding flowers or fruit. The collection is to-day so unique and therefore so valuable, that it has been willed to a museum, but its creation as a collection, was entirely a chance occurrence. The design of a basket trimmed with flowers happened to appeal to the owner, and if we are not mistaken, the now large collection had its beginning in the casual purchase of a little old pendant found in a forgotten corner of Europe. The owner wore it, her friends saw it, and gradually associated the panier fleuri with her, which resulted in many beautiful specimens of this design being sought out for her by wanderers at home and abroad. To-day this collection includes old silks, laces, jewellery, wax pictures, old prints, some pieces of antique furniture, snuffboxes and ornaments in glass, china, silver, etc.

Every museum is the result of fads in collecting, and when one considers all that is meant by this heading, which sounds so trifling and unimportant to the layman, it will not seem strange that we strongly recommend it as a dissipation!

At first, quite naturally, the collector makes mistakes; but it is through his mistakes that he learns, and absolutely nothing gives such a zest to a stroll in the city, a tramp in the country, or an unexpected delay in an out-of-the-way town, as to have this collecting bee in your bonnet. How often when travelling we have rejoiced when the loss of a train or a mistake in time-table, meant an unexpected opportunity to explore for junk in some old shop, or, perhaps, to bargain with a pretty peasant girl who hoarded a beloved heirloom, of entrancing interest to us (and worth a pile of money really), while she lived happily on cider and cheese!

It is doubtless the experience of every lover of the old and the curious, that one never regrets the expenses incurred in this quest of the antique, but one does eternally regret one's economies. The writer suffers now, after years have elapsed, in some cases, at the memory of treasures resisted when chanced upon in Russia, Poland, Hungary, Bohemia—where not! Always one says, "Oh, well, I shall come back again!" But there are so many "pastures green," and it is often difficult to retrace one's steps.

Then, too, these fads open our eyes and ears, so that in passing along a street on foot, in a cab or on a bus, or in glancing through a book, or, perhaps, in an odd corner of an otherwise colourless town, where fate has taken us, we find "grist for our mill"—just the right piece of furniture for the waiting place!

Know what you want, really want it, and you will find it some time, somewhere, somehow!

As a stimulus to beginners in collecting, as well as an illustration of that perseverance required of every keen collector, we cite the case of running down an Empire dressing-table.

It was our desire to complete a small collection of Empire furniture for a suite of rooms, by adding to it as a supplement to the bureau, a certain type of Empire dressing-table. It is no exaggeration to say that Paris was dragged for what we wanted—the large well-known antique shops and the smaller ones of the Latin Quarter being both ransacked. Time was flying, the date of our sailing was approaching, and as yet the coveted piece had not been found. Three days before we left, a fat, red-faced, jolly cabby, after making a vain tour of the junk shops in his quarter, demanded to know exactly what it was we sought. When told, he looked triumphant, bade us get into his cab, lashed his horse and after several rapidly made turns, dashed into an out-of-the-way street and drew up before a sort of junk store-house, full of rickety, dusty odds and ends of furniture, presided over by a stupid old woman who sat outside the door, knitting,—wrapped head and all in a shawl. We entered and, there, to our immense relief, stood the dressing table! It was grey with dust, the original Empire green silk, a rusty grey and hanging in shreds on the back of the original glass. There was a marble top set into the wood and grooved in a curious way. The whole was intact except for a loose back leg, which gave it a swaying, tottering appearance. We passed it in silence—being experienced traders! Then, after buying several little old picture frames, while Madame continued her knitting, we wandered close to the coveted table and asked what was wanted for that broken bit "of no use as it stands."

"Thirty francs" (six dollars) was the answer.

Later a well-known New York dealer offered seventy-five dollars for the table in the condition in which we found it, and repaired as it is to-day it would easily bring a hundred and fifty, anywhere!

As it happened, the money we went out with had been spent on unexpected finds, and neither we nor our good-natured cabby were in possession of thirty francs! In fact, cabby was rather staggered to hear the price, having offered to advance what we needed. He suggested sending it home "collect" but Madame would not even consider such an idea. However, at last our resourceful jehu came to the rescue. If the ladies would seat themselves in the cab, he could place the table in front of them, with the cover of the cab raised, and Madame of the shop could lock her door and mounting the box by the side of our cocher, she might drive with us to our destination and collect the money herself! He promised to bring her home safely again!

As we had only the next day for boxing and shipping, there was no alternative. Before we had even taken in our grotesque appearance, the horse was galloping, as only a Paris cab horse can gallop, toward our abode in Avenue Henri Martin, past carriages and autos returning from the Bois, while inside the cab we sat, elated by our success and in that whirl of triumphant absorbing joy which only the real collector knows.

This same modest little Empire collection had a treasure recently added to it, found by chance, in an antique shop in Pennsylvania. It was a mirror. The dealer, an Italian, said that he had got it from an old house in Bordentown, New Jersey.

"It's genuine English," he said, certain he was playing his winning card.

It has the original glass and a heavy, squarely made, mahogany frame. Strange to say it corresponds exactly with the bed and bureau in the collection, having pilasters surmounted by women's heads of gilded wood with small gilded feet showing at base.

PLATE XXXI

An end of a room containing genuine Empire furniture, Empire ornaments and a rare collection of Empire cups, which appear in a vitrine seen near the dull-blue brocade curtains drawn over windows.

We would especially call attention to the mantelpiece, which was originally the Empire frame of a mirror, and to a book shelf made interesting by having the upper shelf supported by a charming pair of antique bronze cupids.

This plate is reproduced to show as many Empire pieces as possible; it is not an ideal example of arrangement, either as to furniture in room or certain details. There is too much crowding.

A Collection of Empire Furniture, Ornaments and China

As the brother of the great Napoleon, Joseph Bonaparte, king of Spain and Rome, passed many years of his self-imposed exile in

Bordentown, in a house made beautiful with furnishings he brought from France, it is possible this old mirror has an interesting story, if only it could talk! Then, too, it was Bordentown that sheltered a Prince Murat, the relative of Joseph Bonaparte. If it was he who conveyed our mirror to these shores, a very different, but as highly romantic a tale might unfold!

For fear the precious ancient glass should be broken or the frame destroyed, we bribed a Pullman-car porter to let us bring its six by four feet of antiquity with us, in the train!

When you see a find always take it with you, or the next man may, and above all, always be on the lookout.

It was from a French novel by one of the living French writers that we first got a clue to a certain obscure Etruscan museum, hidden away in the Carrara Mountains, in Italy. That wonderful little museum and its adjacent potteries, which cover the face of Italy like ant-hills, are to-day contributors to innumerable beautiful interiors in every part of America.

We recall a dining-room in Grosvenor Square, London, where a world-renowned collection of "powder-blue" vases (the property of Mr. J.B. Joel) is made to contribute to a decorative scheme by placing the almost priceless vases of old Chinese blue and white porcelain, in niches made for them, high up on the black oak panelling. There are no pictures nor other decorations on the walls, hence each vase has the distinction it deserves, placed as it were, in a shrine.

In the Peter Hewitt Museum, New York, you may see an antique Italian china cabinet, made of gilded carved wood, which shows on its undulating front, row after row of small niches, lined with red velvet. When each deep niche held its porcelain chef d'oeuvre, the effect must have been that of a gold screen set with gems!

Speaking of red velvet backgrounds, in the same museum, standing near the Italian cabinet, is an ancient Spanish one; its elaborate steel hinges, locks and ornaments have each a bit of red velvet between them and the oak of the cabinet. One sees this on Gothic chests in England and occasionally on the antique furniture of other countries. The red material stretched back of the metal fretwork, is said to be a souvenir of the gruesome custom prevailing in ancient times, of warning off invaders by posting on the doors of public buildings, the skin of prisoners of war, and holding it in place with open-work metal, through which the red skin was plainly seen!

At Cornwall Lodge, in Regents Park, London, the town house of Lady de Bathe (Lily Langtry) the dining-room ceiling is a deep sky-blue, while the sidewalls of black, serve as a background for her valuable collection of old, coloured glass, for the most part English. The collection is the result of the owner's eternal vigilance, when travelling or at home.

A well-known Paris collector, now dead, found in Spain a bust which had been painted black. Its good lines led him to buy it, and, when cleaned, it proved to be a genuine Canova, and was sold by this dealer, a reliable expert, to an American for five thousand dollars! It had been painted during a Revolution, to save it from destruction.

The same dealer on another occasion, when in Spain, found an old silk gown of lovely flowered brocade, but with one breadth missing. Several years later, in an antique shop in Italy, he found that missing gore and had it put back in the gown, thus completing the treasure which some ruthless hand had destroyed.

CHAPTER XXXIX

WEDGWOOD POTTERY, OLD AND MODERN

Many of our museums have interesting collections of old Wedgwood. Altogether the most complete collection we have ever seen is in the museum adjoining the Wedgwood factories in Staffordshire, England. The curator there, an old man of about seventy, loves to tell the story of its founding and growth. He began as a labourer in the potteries and has worked his way up to be guardian of the veterans in perfected types. Many of the rare and beautiful specimens he has himself dug up in the grounds, where from time to time, since 1750, they were thrown out as broken, useless debris. The recovery of these bits, their preservation and classification, together with valuable donations made by English families who have inherited rare specimens, have not only placed at the disposal of those interested, the fascinating history of Wedgwood, in a thrilling object lesson, but has made the modern Wedgwood what it is:—one of the most beautiful varieties of tableware in the market to-day.

Josiah Wedgwood is said to have been the first English potter, counting from the Roman time to the first quarter of the eighteenth century, who made vases to be used for mere decoration. Chelsea, Worcester and Derby were just then beginning to make fine porcelain. In Wedgwood's day it was the rule for young men of title and wealth to go abroad, and the souvenirs which they brought back with them, such as pictures and vases, helped to form a taste for the antique, in England. Then, too, books on Greek art were being written by English travellers. Josiah Wedgwood had a natural bent for the pure line and classic subjects, but he was, also, possessed with the keen businessman's intuition as to what his particular market demanded. So he sat about copying the line and decorations of the antique Greek vases. He reproduced lines and designs in decoration, but invented the "bodies," that is to say, the materials from which the potters moulded his wares. He is said to have invented in all, twenty varieties. We say that he reproduced Greek designs, and so he did, but John Flaxman, his chief decorator, who lived in Rome, where he had a studio and clever assistants, studied the classics, imbibed their spirit and originated the large majority of Wedgwood's so-called "Greek" designs,—those exquisite cameo-like compositions in white, on backgrounds of pastel colours, which appeared as miniatures mounted for jewellery, medallions let into wall panels, and on furniture and Carrara marble mantelpieces, wonderful works of art wrought of his "Jasper" paste, which make Josiah Wedgwood outrank any producer of ceramics who has ever lived in any age.

Wedgwood's first vases were for use, although they were ornamental, too. Those were the pots he made in which to grow bulbs or roots, and the "bough pots" which were filled with cut flowers and used to ornament the hearth in summer.

Mr. Frederick Rathbone, compiler of the Wedgwood catalogue in 1909, a memorial to Josiah Wedgwood made possible by his great-granddaughter, says that during his thirty-five years' study of Wedgwood's work, he had yet to learn of a single vase which was ever made by him, or sent out from his factory at Etruria, which was lacking in grace or beauty.

The Etrurian Museum, Staffordshire, shows Josiah Wedgwood's life work from the early Whieldon ware to his perfected Jasper paste. Josiah's "trials" or experiments, are the most interesting specimens in the museum, and prove that the effort of his life was "converting a rude and inconsiderable manufactory into an elegant art and an important part of national commerce." Yet, although he is acknowledged by all the world to have been the greatest artist in ceramics of his or any period, remember pottery was only one of his interests. He was by no means a man who concentrated day and night on one line of production. He occupied himself with politics, and planned and carried through great engineering feats and was, also, deeply interested in the education of his children.

When Wedgwood began his work, all tea and coffee pots were "salt-glazed," plain, or, if decorated, copies of Oriental patterns, which were the only available models, imported for the use of the rich. Wedgwood invented in turn his tortoise shell, agate, mottled and other coloured wares, and finally his beautiful pale-cream, known as "Queen's" ware, in honour of Queen Charlotte, his patron. It is the "C.C." (cream colour) which is so popular to-day, either plain or decorated. He invented colours, as well as bodies, for the manufacture of his earthenware, both for use and for decoration, and built up a business employing 15,000 persons in his factories,— and 30,000 in all the branches of his business.

In 1896 the census showed 45,914 persons employed in the factories, and at that time the annual amount paid in wages was over two million pounds (ten million dollars).

We must remember that in 1760, the only way of transporting goods to and from the Wedgwood factory was by means of packhorses. Therefore Josiah Wedgwood had to turn his attention to the construction of roads and canals. As Mr. Gladstone put it in his address at the opening of the Wedgwood Institute at Burslem, Staffordshire, "Wedgwood made the raw material of his industry abundant and cheap, which supplied a vent for the manufactured article and which opened for it materially a way to what we may term the conquest of the outer world." Yet he never travelled outside his own country; always employed English workmen to carry out his ideas, and succeeded entirely by his own efforts, unaided by the state. His first patroness was Catherine II of Russia, for whom he made a wonderful table service, and his best customers were the court and aristocracy of France, during that country's greatest art periods (Louis XV and XVI). In fact Wedgwood ware became so fashionable in Paris that the Sèvres, Royal Porcelain factory, copied the colour and relief of his Jasper plaques and vases. It is claimed by connoisseurs, that the Wedgwood useful decorative pottery is the only ceramic art in which England is supreme and unassailable.

It has been said at the Wedgwood works, and with great pride, that the copying of Wedgwood by the Sèvres factories, and the preservation of many rare examples of his work to-day, in French museums, to serve as models for French designers and craftsman, is a neat compliment to the English—"those rude islanders with three hundred religions and only one sauce"!

PLATE XXXII

In the illustration five of the four vases, four with covers and one without, are reproductions of old pharmacy jars, once used by all Italian druggists to keep their drugs in.

The really old ones with artistic worth are vanishing from the open market into knowing dealers' or collectors' hands, or the museums have them, but with true Latin perspicuity, when the supply ceased to meet the demand, the great modern Italian potters turned out lovely reproductions, so lovely that they bring high prices in Italy as well as abroad, and are frequently offered to collectors when in Italy as genuine antiques.

Italian Reproductions in Pottery after Classic Models

CHAPTER XL

ITALIAN POTTERY

About nine years ago, an American connoisseur, automobiling from Paris to Vienna, the route which lies through Northern Italy, quite by chance, happened to see some statuettes in the window of a hopeful, but unknown, potter's little shop, on a wonderful, ancient, covered bridge. You, too, may have seen that rarely beautiful bridge spanning the River Brenta, and have looked out through broad arches which occur at intervals, on views, so extraordinary that one feels they must be on a Gothic tapestry, or the journey just a dream! One cannot forget the wild, rushing river of purplish-blues, and the pines, in deep greens, which climb up, past ruined castles, perched on jutting rocks, toward snow-capped mountain peaks. The views were beautiful, but so were the statuettes which had caught our collector's eye. He bought some, made inquiries as to facilities for reproduction at these potteries, and exchanged addresses. The result was that to-day, that humble potter directs several large factories, which are busy reviving classic designs, which may be found on sale everywhere in Italy and in many other countries as well as America.

CHAPTER XLI

VENETIAN GLASS, OLD AND MODERN

If you have been in Venice then you know the Murano Museum and its beguiling collection of Venetian glass, that old glass so vastly more beautiful in line and decoration than the modern type of, say, fifteen years ago, when colours had become bad mixtures, and decorations meaningless excrescences.

A bit of inside information given out to some one really interested, led to a revival of pure line and lovely, simple colouring, with appropriate decorations or none at all. You may already know that romantic bit of history. It seems that when the museum was first started, about four hundred years ago, the glass blowers agreed to donate specimens of their work, provided their descendants should be allowed access to the museum for models. This contract made it a simple matter for a connoisseur to get reproduced exactly what was wanted, and what was not in the market. Elegance, distinguished simplicity in shapes, done in glass of a single colour, or in one colour with a simple edge in a contrasting shade, or in one colour with a whole nosegay of colours to set it off, appearing literally as flowers or fruit to surmount the stopper of a bottle, the top of a jar, or as decorations on candlesticks.

It was in the Museo Civico of Venice that we saw and fell victims to an enchanting antique table decoration—a formal Italian garden, in blown glass, once the property of a great Venetian family and redolent of those golden days when Venice was the playground of princes, and feasting their especial joy; days when visiting royalty and the world's greatest folk could have no higher honour bestowed upon them than a gift of Venetian glass, often real marvels mounted in silver and gold.

We never tired of looking at that fairy garden with its delicate copings, balustrades and vases of glass, all abloom with exquisite posies in every conceivable shade, wrought of glass—a veritable dream thing! Finally, nothing would do but we must know if it had ever been copied. The curator said that he believed it had, and an address was given us. How it all comes back! We arose at dawn, as time was precious, took our coffee in haste and then came that gliding trip in the gondola, through countless canals, to a quarter quite unknown to us, where at work in a small room, we came upon our glass blower and the coveted copy of that lovely table-garden. This man had made four, and one was still in his possession. We brought it back to America, a gleaming jewelled cobweb, and what happened was that the very ethereal quality of its beauty made the average taste ignore it! However, a few years have made a vast difference in table, as well as all other decorations, and to-day the same Venetian gardens have their faithful devotees, as is proved by the continuous procession of the dainty wonders, ever moving toward our sturdy shores.

IN CONCLUSION

In bringing our book to an end we would reiterate four fundamental principles of Interior Decoration (and all decoration):

Good lines.

Correct proportions.

Harmonious colour scheme (which includes the question of background) and Appropriateness.

Observe these four laws and any house, all interior decoration, and any lawn or garden, will be beautiful and satisfying, regardless of type and choice of colours.

Whether or not you remain content with your achievement depends upon your mental makeup. Really know what you want as a home, want it, and you can work out any scheme, provided you have intelligence, patience and perseverance.

To learn what is meant by good line, one must educate oneself by making a point of seeing beautiful furniture and furnishings. Visit museums, all collections which boast the stamp of approval of experts; buy at the best modern and antique shops, and compare what you get with the finest examples in the museums. This is the way that connaisseurs are made.